Memories of an Indian Boyhood

Charles A. Eastman

T0164687

MINT EDITIONS

Memories of an Indian Boyhood was first published in 1902.

This edition published by Mint Editions 2021.

ISBN 9781513283319 | E-ISBN 9781513288338

Published by Mint Editions®

 MINT
EDITIONS

minteditionbooks.com

Publishing Director: Jennifer Newens
Design & Production: Rachel Lopez Metzger
Project Manager: Micaela Clark
Typesetting: Westchester Publishing Services

Contents

I

Earliest Recollections

I. Hakadah, "The Pitiful Last"

WHAT BOY WOULD NOT BE an Indian for a while when he thinks of the freest life in the world? This life was mine. Every day there was a real hunt. There was real game. Occasionally there was a medicine dance away off in the woods where no one could disturb us, in which the boys impersonated their elders, Brave Bull, Standing Elk, High Hawk, Medicine Bear, and the rest. They painted and imitated their fathers and grandfathers to the minutest detail, and accurately too, because they had seen the real thing all their lives.

We were not only good mimics but we were close students of nature. We studied the habits of animals just as you study your books. We watched the men of our people and represented them in our play; then learned to emulate them in our lives.

No people have a better use of their five senses than the children of the wilderness. We could smell as well as hear and see. We could feel and taste as well as we could see and hear. Nowhere has the memory been more fully developed than in the wild life, and I can still see wherein I owe much to my early training.

Of course I myself do not remember when I first saw the day, but my brothers have often recalled the event with much mirth; for it was a custom of the Sioux that when a boy was born his brother must plunge into the water, or roll in the snow naked if it was winter time; and if he was not big enough to do either of these himself, water was thrown on him. If the newborn had a sister, she must be immersed. The idea was that a warrior had come to camp, and the other children must display some act of hardihood.

I was so unfortunate as to be the youngest of five children who, soon after I was born, were left motherless. I had to bear the humiliating name "Hakadah," meaning "the pitiful last," until I should earn a more dignified and appropriate name. I was regarded as little more than a plaything by the rest of the children.

My mother, who was known as the handsomest woman of all the Spirit Lake and Leaf Dweller Sioux, was dangerously ill, and one of the medicine men who attended her said: "Another medicine man has come into existence, but the mother must die. Therefore let him bear the name 'Mysterious Medicine.'" But one of the bystanders hastily interfered, saying that an uncle of the child already bore that name, so, for the time, I was only "Hakadah."

My beautiful mother, sometimes called the "Demi-Goddess" of the Sioux, who tradition says had every feature of a Caucasian descent with the exception of her luxuriant black hair and deep black eyes, held me tightly to her bosom upon her death-bed, while she whispered a few words to her mother-in-law. She said: "I give you this boy for your own. I cannot trust my own mother with him; she will neglect him and he will surely die."

The woman to whom these words were spoken was below the average in stature, remarkably active for her age (she was then fully sixty), and possessed of as much goodness as intelligence. My mother's judgment concerning her own mother was well founded, for soon after her death that old lady appeared, and declared that Hakadah was too young to live without a mother. She offered to keep me until I died, and then she would put me in my mother's grave. Of course my other grandmother denounced the suggestion as a very wicked one, and refused to give me up.

The babe was done up as usual in a movable cradle made from an oak board two and a half feet long and one and a half feet wide. On one side of it was nailed with brass-headed tacks the richly-embroidered sack, which was open in front and laced up and down with buckskin strings. Over the arms of the infant was a wooden bow, the ends of which were firmly attached to the board, so that if the cradle should fall the child's head and face would be protected. On this bow were hung curious playthings—strings of artistically carved bones and hoofs of deer, which rattled when the little hands moved them.

In this upright cradle I lived, played and slept the greater part of the time during the first few months of my life. Whether I was made to lean against a lodge pole or was suspended from a bough of a tree, while my grandmother cut wood, or whether I was carried on her back, or conveniently balanced by another child in a similar cradle hung on the opposite side of a pony, I was still in my oaken bed.

This grandmother, who had already lived through sixty years of hardships, was a wonder to the young maidens of the tribe. She showed no less enthusiasm over Hakadah than she had done when she held her first-born, the boy's father, in her arms. Every little attention that is due to a loved child she performed with much skill and devotion. She made all my scanty garments and my tiny moccasins with a great deal of taste. It was said by all that I could not have had more attention had my mother been living.

Uncheedah (grandmother) was a great singer. Sometimes, when Hakadah wakened too early in the morning, she would sing to him something like the following lullaby:

Sleep, sleep, my boy, the Chippewas
Are far away—are far away.
Sleep, sleep, my boy; prepare to meet
The foe by day—the foe by day!
The cowards will not dare to fight
Till morning break—till morning break.
Sleep, sleep, my child, while still 'tis night;
Then bravely wake—then bravely wake!

The Dakota women were wont to cut and bring their fuel from the woods and, in fact, to perform most of the drudgery of the camp. This of necessity fell to their lot, because the men must follow the game during the day. Very often my grandmother carried me with her on these excursions; and while she worked it was her habit to suspend me from a wild grape vine or a springy bough, so that the least breeze would swing the cradle to and fro.

She has told me that when I had grown old enough to take notice, I was apparently capable of holding extended conversations in an unknown dialect with birds and red squirrels. Once I fell asleep in my cradle, suspended five or six feet from the ground, while Uncheedah was some distance away, gathering birch bark for a canoe. A squirrel had found it convenient to come upon the bow of my cradle and nibble his hickory nut, until he awoke me by dropping the crumbs of his meal. My disapproval of his intrusion was so decided that he had to take a sudden and quick flight to another bough, and from there he began to pour out his wrath upon me, while I continued my objections to his presence so audibly that Uncheedah soon came to my rescue, and compelled the bold intruder to go away. It was a common thing for birds to alight on my cradle in the woods.

My food was, at first, a troublesome question for my kind foster-mother. She cooked some wild rice and strained it, and mixed it with broth made from choice venison. She also pounded dried venison almost to a flour, and kept it in water till the nourishing juices were extracted, then mixed with it some pounded maize, which was browned before pounding. This soup of wild rice, pounded venison and maize was my main-stay. But soon my teeth came—much earlier than the white children usually cut theirs; and then my good nurse gave me a little more varied food, and I did all my own grinding.

After I left my cradle, I almost walked away from it, she told me. She then began calling my attention to natural objects. Whenever I heard the song of a bird, she would tell me what bird it came from, something after this fashion:

"Hakadah, listen to Shechoka (the robin) calling his mate. He says he has just found something good to eat." Or "Listen to Oopehanska (the thrush); he is singing for his little wife. He will sing his best." When in the evening the whippoorwill started his song with vim, no further than a stone's throw from our tent in the woods, she would say to me:

"Hush! It may be an Ojibway scout!"

Again, when I waked at midnight, she would say:

"Do not cry! Hinakaga (the owl) is watching you from the tree-top."

I usually covered up my head, for I had perfect faith in my grandmother's admonitions, and she had given me a dreadful idea of this bird. It was one of her legends that a little boy was once standing just outside of the teepee (tent), crying vigorously for his mother, when Hinakaga swooped down in the darkness and carried the poor little fellow up into the trees. It was well known that the hoot of the owl was commonly imitated by Indian scouts when on the war-path. There had been dreadful massacres immediately following this call. Therefore it was deemed wise to impress the sound early upon the mind of the child.

Indian children were trained so that they hardly ever cried much in the night. This was very expedient and necessary in their exposed life. In my infancy it was my grandmother's custom to put me to sleep, as she said, with the birds, and to waken me with them, until it became a habit. She did this with an object in view. An Indian must always rise early. In the first place, as a hunter, he finds his game best at daybreak. Secondly, other tribes, when on the war-path, usually make their attack very early in the morning. Even when our people are moving about leisurely, we like to rise before daybreak, in order to travel when the air is cool, and unobserved, perchance, by our enemies.

As a little child, it was instilled into me to be silent and reticent. This was one of the most important traits to form in the character of the Indian. As a hunter and warrior it was considered absolutely necessary to him, and was thought to lay the foundations of patience and self-control. There are times when boisterous mirth is indulged in by our people, but the rule is gravity and decorum.

After all, my babyhood was full of interest and the beginnings of life's realities. The spirit of daring was already whispered into my ears. The value of the eagle feather as worn by the warrior had caught my eye. One day, when I was left alone, at scarcely two years of age, I took my uncle's war bonnet and plucked out all its eagle feathers to decorate my dog and myself. So soon the life that was about me had made its impress, and already I desired intensely to comply with all of its demands.

II. Early Hardships

ONE OF THE EARLIEST RECOLLECTIONS of my adventurous childhood is the ride I had on a pony's side. I was passive in the whole matter. A little girl cousin of mine was put in a bag and suspended from the horn of an Indian saddle; but her weight must be balanced or the saddle would not remain on the animal's back. Accordingly, I was put into another sack and made to keep the saddle and the girl in position! I did not object at all, for I had a very pleasant game of peek-aboo with the little girl, until we came to a big snow-drift, where the poor beast was stuck fast and began to lie down. Then it was not so nice!

This was the convenient and primitive way in which some mothers packed their children for winter journeys. However cold the weather might be, the inmate of the fur-lined sack was usually very comfortable—at least I used to think so. I believe I was accustomed to all the precarious Indian conveyances, and, as a boy, I enjoyed the dog-travaux ride as much as any. The travaux consisted of a set of rawhide strips securely lashed to the tent-poles, which were harnessed to the sides of the animal as if he stood between shafts, while the free ends were allowed to drag on the ground. Both ponies and large dogs were used as beasts of burden, and they carried in this way the smaller children as well as the baggage.

This mode of travelling for children was possible only in the summer, and as the dogs were sometimes unreliable, the little ones were exposed to a certain amount of danger. For instance, whenever a train of dogs had been travelling for a long time, almost perishing with the heat and their heavy loads, a glimpse of water would cause them to forget all their responsibilities. Some of them, in spite of the screams of the women, would swim with their burdens into the cooling stream, and I was thus, on more than one occasion, made to partake of an unwilling bath.

I was a little over four years old at the time of the "Sioux massacre" in Minnesota. In the general turmoil, we took flight into British Columbia, and the journey is still vividly remembered by all our family. A yoke of oxen and a lumber-wagon were taken from some white farmer and brought home for our conveyance.

How delighted I was when I learned that we were to ride behind those wise-looking animals and in that gorgeously painted wagon! It seemed almost like a living creature to me, this new vehicle with four legs, and the more so when we got out of axle-grease and the wheels went along squealing like pigs!

The boys found a great deal of innocent fun in jumping from the high wagon while the oxen were leisurely moving along. My elder brothers soon became experts. At last, I mustered up courage enough to join them in this sport. I was sure they stepped on the wheel, so I cautiously placed my moccasined foot upon it. Alas! before I could realize what had happened, I was under the wheels, and had it not been for the neighbor immediately behind us, I might have been run over by the next team as well.

This was my first experience with a civilized vehicle. I cried out all possible reproaches on the white man's team and concluded that a dog-travaux was good enough for me. I was really rejoiced that we were moving away from the people who made the wagon that had almost ended my life, and it did not occur to me that I alone was to blame. I could not be persuaded to ride in that wagon again and was glad when we finally left it beside the Missouri river.

The summer after the "Minnesota massacre," General Sibley pursued our people across this river. Now the Missouri is considered one of the most treacherous rivers in the world. Even a good modern boat is not safe upon its uncertain current. We were forced to cross in buffalo-skin boats—as round as tubs!

The Washechu (white men) were coming in great numbers with their big guns, and while most of our men were fighting them to gain time, the women and the old men made and equipped the temporary boats, braced with ribs of willow. Some of these were towed by two or three women or men swimming in the water and some by ponies. It was not an easy matter to keep them right side up, with their helpless freight of little children and such goods as we possessed.

In our flight, we little folks were strapped in the saddles or held in front of an older person, and in the long night marches to get away from the soldiers, we suffered from loss of sleep and insufficient food. Our meals were eaten hastily, and sometimes in the saddle. Water was not always to be found. The people carried it with them in bags formed of tripe or the dried pericardium of animals.

Now we were compelled to trespass upon the country of hostile tribes and were harassed by them almost daily and nightly. Only the strictest vigilance saved us.

One day we met with another enemy near the British lines. It was a prairie fire. We were surrounded. Another fire was quickly made, which saved our lives.

One of the most thrilling experiences of the following winter was a blizzard, which overtook us in our wanderings. Here and there, a family lay down in the snow, selecting a place where it was not likely to drift much. For a day and a night we lay under the snow. Uncle stuck a long pole beside us to tell us when the storm was over. We had plenty of buffalo robes and the snow kept us warm, but we found it heavy. After a time, it became packed and hollowed out around our bodies, so that we were as comfortable as one can be under those circumstances.

The next day the storm ceased, and we discovered a large herd of buffaloes almost upon us. We dug our way out, shot some of the buffaloes, made a fire and enjoyed a good dinner.

I was now an exile as well as motherless; yet I was not unhappy. Our wanderings from place to place afforded us many pleasant experiences and quite as many hardships and misfortunes. There were times of plenty and times of scarcity, and we had several narrow escapes from death. In savage life, the early spring is the most trying time and almost all the famines occurred at this period of the year.

The Indians are a patient and a clannish people; their love for one another is stronger than that of any civilized people I know. If this were not so, I believe there would have been tribes of cannibals among them.

White people have been known to kill and eat their companions in preference to starving; but Indians—never!

In times of famine, the adults often denied themselves in order to make the food last as long as possible for the children, who were not able to bear hunger as well as the old. As a people, they can live without food much longer than any other nation.

I once passed through one of these hard springs when we had nothing to eat for several days. I well remember the six small birds which constituted the breakfast for six families one morning; and then we had no dinner or supper to follow! What a relief that was to me—although I had only a small wing of a small bird for my share! Soon after this, we came into a region where buffaloes were plenty, and hunger and scarcity were forgotten.

Such was the Indian's wild life! When game was to be had and the sun shone, they easily forgot the bitter experiences of the winter before. Little preparation was made for the future. They are children of Nature, and occasionally she whips them with the lashes of experience, yet they are forgetful and careless. Much of their suffering might have been prevented by a little calculation.

During the summer, when Nature is at her best, and provides abundantly for the savage, it seems to me that no life is happier than his! Food is free—lodging free—everything free! All were alike rich in the summer, and, again, all were alike poor in the winter and early spring. However, their diseases were fewer and not so destructive as now, and the Indian's health was generally good. The Indian boy enjoyed such a life as almost all boys dream of and would choose for themselves if they were permitted to do so.

The raids made upon our people by other tribes were frequent, and we had to be constantly on the watch. I remember at one time a night attack was made upon our camp and all our ponies stampeded. Only a few of them were recovered, and our journeys after this misfortune were effected mostly by means of the dog-travaux.

The second winter after the massacre, my father and my two older brothers, with several others, were betrayed by a half-breed at Winnipeg to the United States authorities. As I was then living with my uncle in another part of the country, I became separated from them for ten years. During all this time we believed that they had been killed by the whites, and I was taught that I must avenge their deaths as soon as I was able to go upon the war-path.

I must say a word in regard to the character of this uncle, my father's brother, who was my adviser and teacher for many years. He was a man about six feet two inches in height, very erect and broad-shouldered. He was known at that time as one of the best hunters and bravest warriors among the Sioux in British America, where he still lives, for to this day we have failed to persuade him to return to the United States.

He is a typical Indian—not handsome, but truthful and brave. He had a few simple principles from which he hardly ever departed. Some of these I shall describe when I speak of my early training.

It is wonderful that any children grew up through all the exposures and hardships that we suffered in those days! The frail teepee pitched anywhere, in the winter as well as in the summer, was all the protection that we had against cold and storms. I can recall times when we were snowed in and it was very difficult to get fuel. We were once three days without much fire and all of this time it stormed violently. There seemed to be no special anxiety on the part of our people; they rather looked upon all this as a matter of course, knowing that the storm would cease when the time came.

I could once endure as much cold and hunger as any of them; but now if I miss one meal or accidentally wet my feet, I feel it as much as if I had never lived in the manner I have described, when it was a matter of course to get myself soaking wet many a time. Even if there was plenty to eat, it was thought better for us to practice fasting sometimes; and hard exercise was kept up continually, both for the sake of health and to prepare the body for the extraordinary exertions that it might, at any moment, be required to undergo. In my own remembrance, my uncle used often to bring home a deer on his shoulder. The distance was sometimes considerable; yet he did not consider it any sort of a feat.

The usual custom with us was to eat only two meals a day and these were served at each end of the day. This rule was not invariable, however, for if there should be any callers, it was Indian etiquette to offer either tobacco or food, or both. The rule of two meals a day was more closely observed by the men—especially the younger men—than by the women and children. This was when the Indians recognized that a true manhood, one of physical activity and endurance, depends upon dieting and regular exercise. No such system is practised by the reservation Indians of today.

III. My Indian Grandmother

As a motherless child, I always regarded my good grandmother as the wisest of guides and the best of protectors. It was not long before I began to realize her superiority to most of her contemporaries. This idea was not gained entirely from my own observation, but also from a knowledge of the high regard in which she was held by other women. Aside from her native talent and ingenuity, she was endowed with a truly wonderful memory. No other midwife in her day and tribe could compete with her in skill and judgment. Her observations in practice were all preserved in her mind for reference, as systematically as if they had been written upon the pages of a note-book.

I distinctly recall one occasion when she took me with her into the woods in search of certain medicinal roots.

"Why do you not use all kinds of roots for medicines?" said I.

"Because," she replied, in her quick, characteristic manner, "the Great Mystery does not will us to find things too easily. In that case everybody would be a medicine-giver, and Ohiyesa must learn that there are many secrets which the Great Mystery will disclose only to the most worthy. Only those who seek him fasting and in solitude will receive his signs."

With this and many similar explanations she wrought in my soul wonderful and lively conceptions of the "Great Mystery" and of the effects of prayer and solitude. I continued my childish questioning.

"But why did you not dig those plants that we saw in the woods, of the same kind that you are digging now?"

"For the same reason that we do not like the berries we find in the shadow of deep woods as well as the ones which grow in sunny places. The latter have more sweetness and flavor. Those herbs which have medicinal virtues should be sought in a place that is neither too wet nor too dry, and where they have a generous amount of sunshine to maintain their vigor.

"Some day Ohiyesa will be old enough to know the secrets of medicine; then I will tell him all. But if you should grow up to be a bad man, I must withhold these treasures from you and give them to your brother, for a medicine man must be a good and wise man. I hope Ohiyesa will be a great medicine man when he grows up. To be a great warrior is a noble ambition; but to be a mighty medicine man is a nobler!"

She said these things so thoughtfully and impressively that I cannot but feel and remember them even to this day.

Our native women gathered all the wild rice, roots, berries and fruits which formed an important part of our food. This was distinctively a woman's work. Uncheedah (grandmother) understood these matters perfectly, and it became a kind of instinct with her to know just where to look for each edible variety and at what season of the year. This sort of labor gave the Indian women every opportunity to observe and study Nature after their fashion; and in this Uncheedah was more acute than most of the men. The abilities of her boys were not all inherited from their father; indeed, the stronger family traits came obviously from her. She was a leader among the native women, and they came to her, not only for medical aid, but for advice in all their affairs.

In bravery she equaled any of the men. This trait, together with her ingenuity and alertness of mind, more than once saved her and her people from destruction. Once, when we were roaming over a region occupied by other tribes, and on a day when most of the men were out upon the hunt, a party of hostile Indians suddenly appeared. Although there were a few men left at home, they were taken by surprise at first and scarcely knew what to do, when this woman came forward and advanced alone to meet our foes. She had gone some distance when some of the men followed her. She met the strangers and offered her hand to them. They accepted her friendly greeting; and as a result of her brave act we were left unmolested and at peace.

Another story of her was related to me by my father. My grandfather, who was a noted hunter, often wandered away from his band in search of game. In this instance he had with him only his own family of three boys and his wife. One evening, when he returned from the chase, he found to his surprise that she had built a stockade around her teepee.

She had discovered the danger-sign in a single foot-print, which she saw at a glance was not that of her husband, and she was also convinced that it was not the foot-print of a Sioux, from the shape of the moccasin. This ability to recognize footprints is general among the Indians, but more marked in certain individuals.

This courageous woman had driven away a party of five Ojibway warriors. They approached the lodge cautiously, but her dog gave timely warning, and she poured into them from behind her defences the contents of a double-barrelled gun, with such good effect that the astonished braves thought it wise to retreat.

I was not more than five or six years old when the Indian soldiers came one day and destroyed our large buffalo-skin teepee. It was charged that my uncle had hunted alone a large herd of buffaloes. This was not exactly true. He had unfortunately frightened a large herd while shooting a deer in the edge of the woods. However, it was customary to punish such an act severely, even though the offense was accidental.

When we were attacked by the police, I was playing in the teepee, and the only other person at home was Uncheedah. I had not noticed their approach, and when the war-cry was given by thirty or forty Indians with strong lungs, I thought my little world was coming to an end. Instantly innumerable knives and tomahawks penetrated our frail home, while bullets went through the poles and tent-fastenings up above our heads.

I hardly know what I did, but I imagine it was just what any other little fellow would have done under like circumstances. My first clear realization of the situation was when Uncheedah had a dispute with the leader, claiming that the matter had not been properly investigated, and that none of the policemen had attained to a reputation in war which would justify them in touching her son's teepee. But alas! our poor dwelling was already an unrecognizable ruin; even the poles were broken into splinters.

The Indian women, after reaching middle age, are usually heavy and lack agility, but my grandmother was in this also an exception. She was fully sixty when I was born; and when I was seven years old she swam across a swift and wide stream, carrying me on her back, because she did not wish to expose me to accident in one of the clumsy round boats of bull-hide which were rigged up to cross the rivers which impeded our way, especially in the springtime. Her strength and endurance were remarkable. Even after she had attained the age of eighty-two, she one day walked twenty-five miles without appearing much fatigued.

I marvel now at the purity and elevated sentiment possessed by this woman, when I consider the customs and habits of her people at the time. When her husband died she was still comparatively a young woman—still active, clever and industrious. She was descended from a haughty chieftain of the "Dwellers among the Leaves." Although women of her age and position were held to be eligible to re-marriage, and she had several persistent suitors who were men of her own age and chiefs, yet she preferred to cherish in solitude the memory of her husband.

I was very small when my uncle brought home two Ojibway young women. In the fight in which they were captured, none of the Sioux war party had been killed; therefore they were sympathized with and tenderly treated by the Sioux women. They were apparently happy, although of course they felt deeply the losses sustained at the time of their capture, and they did not fail to show their appreciation of the kindnesses received at our hands.

As I recall now the remarks made by one of them at the time of their final release, they appear to me quite remarkable. They lived in my grandmother's family for two years, and were then returned to their people at a great peace council of the two nations. When they were about to leave my grandmother, the elder of the two sisters first embraced her, and then spoke somewhat as follows:

"You are a brave woman and a true mother. I understand now why your son so bravely conquered our band, and took my sister and myself captive. I hated him at first, but now I admire him, because he did just what my father, my brother or my husband would have done had they opportunity. He did even more. He saved us from the tomahawks of his fellow-warriors, and brought us to his home to know a noble and a brave woman.

"I shall never forget your many favors shown to us. But I must go. I belong to my tribe and I shall return to them. I will endeavor to be a true woman also, and to teach my boys to be generous warriors like your son."

Her sister chose to remain among the Sioux all her life, and she married one of our young men.

"I shall make the Sioux and the Ojibways," she said, "to be as brothers."

There are many other instances of intermarriage with captive women. The mother of the well-known Sioux chieftain, Wabashaw, was an Ojibway woman. I once knew a woman who was said to be a white captive. She was married to a noted warrior, and had a fine family of five boys. She was well accustomed to the Indian ways, and as a child I should not have suspected that she was white. The skins of these people became so sunburned and full of paint that it required a keen eye to distinguish them from the real Indians.

IV. An Indian Sugar Camp

WITH THE FIRST MARCH THAW the thoughts of the Indian women of my childhood days turned promptly to the annual sugarmaking.

This industry was chiefly followed by the old men and women and the children. The rest of the tribe went out upon the spring fur-hunt at this season, leaving us at home to make the sugar.

The first and most important of the necessary utensils were the huge iron and brass kettles for boiling. Everything else could be made, but these must be bought, begged or borrowed. A maple tree was felled and a log canoe hollowed out, into which the sap was to be gathered. Little troughs of basswood and birchen basins were also made to receive the sweet drops as they trickled from the tree.

As soon as these labors were accomplished, we all proceeded to the bark sugar house, which stood in the midst of a fine grove of maples on the bank of the Minnesota river. We found this hut partially filled with the snows of winter and the withered leaves of the preceding autumn, and it must be cleared for our use. In the meantime a tent was pitched outside for a few days' occupancy. The snow was still deep in the woods, with a solid crust upon which we could easily walk; for we usually moved to the sugar house before the sap had actually started, the better to complete our preparations.

My grandmother worked like a beaver in these days (or rather like a muskrat, as the Indians say; for this industrious little animal sometimes collects as many as six or eight bushels of edible roots for the winter, only to be robbed of his store by some of our people). If there was prospect of a good sugaring season, she now made a second and even a third canoe to contain the sap. These canoes were afterward utilized by the hunters for their proper purpose.

During our last sugar-making in Minnesota, before the "outbreak," my grandmother was at work upon a canoe with her axe, while a young aunt of mine stood by. We boys were congregated within the large, oval sugar house, busily engaged in making arrows for the destruction of the rabbits and chipmunks which we knew would come in numbers to drink the sap. The birds also were beginning to return, and the cold storms of March would drive them to our door. I was then too young to do much except look on; but I fully entered into the spirit of the occasion, and rejoiced to see the bigger boys industriously sharpen their arrows, resting them against the ends of the long sticks which were burning in the fire, and occasionally cutting a chip from the stick. In their eagerness they paid little attention to this circumstance, although they well knew that it was strictly forbidden to touch a knife to a burning ember.

CHARLES A. EASTMAN

Suddenly loud screams were heard from without and we all rushed out to see what was the matter. It was a serious affair. My grandmother's axe had slipped, and by an upward stroke nearly severed three of the fingers of my aunt, who stood looking on, with her hands folded upon her waist. As we ran out the old lady, who had already noticed and reproved our carelessness in regard to the burning embers, pursued us with loud reproaches and threats of a whipping. This will seem mysterious to my readers, but is easily explained by the Indian superstition, which holds that such an offense as we had committed is invariably punished by the accidental cutting of some one of the family.

My grandmother did not confine herself to canoe-making. She also collected a good supply of fuel for the fires, for she would not have much time to gather wood when the sap began to flow. Presently the weather moderated and the snow began to melt. The month of April brought showers which carried most of it off into the Minnesota river. Now the women began to test the trees-moving leisurely among them, axe in hand, and striking a single quick blow, to see if the sap would appear. The trees, like people, have their individual characters; some were ready to yield up their life-blood, while others were more reluctant. Now one of the birchen basins was set under each tree, and a hardwood chip driven deep into the cut which the axe had made. From the corners of this chip—at first drop by drop, then more freely-the sap trickled into the little dishes.

It is usual to make sugar from maples, but several other trees were also tapped by the Indians. From the birch and ash was made a dark-colored sugar, with a somewhat bitter taste, which was used for medicinal purposes. The box-elder yielded a beautiful white sugar, whose only fault was that there was never enough of it!

A long fire was now made in the sugar house, and a row of brass kettles suspended over the blaze. The sap was collected by the women in tin or birchen buckets and poured into the canoes, from which the kettles were kept filled. The hearts of the boys beat high with pleasant anticipations when they heard the welcome hissing sound of the boiling sap! Each boy claimed one kettle for his especial charge. It was his duty to see that the fire was kept up under it, to watch lest it boil over, and finally, when the sap became sirup, to test it upon the snow, dipping it out with a wooden paddle. So frequent were these tests that for the first day or two we consumed nearly all that could be made; and it was not until the sweetness began to pall that my grandmother set herself in earnest to store up sugar for future use. She made it into cakes of various forms, in birchen molds, and sometimes in hollow canes or reeds, and the bills of ducks and geese. Some of it was pulverized and packed in rawhide cases. Being a prudent woman, she did not give it to us after the first month or so, except upon special occasions, and it was thus made to last almost the year around. The smaller candies were reserved as an occasional treat for the little fellows, and the sugar was eaten at feasts with wild rice or parched corn, and also with pounded dried meat. Coffee and tea, with their substitutes, were all unknown to us in those days.

Every pursuit has its trials and anxieties. My grandmother's special tribulations, during the sugaring season, were the upsetting and gnawing of holes in her birch-bark pans. The transgressors were the rabbit and squirrel tribes, and we little boys for once became useful, in shooting them with our bows and arrows. We hunted all over the sugar camp, until the little creatures were fairly driven out of the neighborhood. Occasionally one of my older brothers brought home a rabbit or two, and then we had a feast.

The sugaring season extended well into April, and the returning birds made the precincts of our camp joyful with their songs. I often followed my older brothers into the woods, although I was then but four or five years old. Upon one of these excursions they went so far that I ventured back alone. When within sight of our hut, I saw a chipmunk sitting upon a log, and uttering the sound he makes when he calls to his mate. How glorious it would be, I thought, if I could shoot him with my tiny bow and arrows! Stealthily and cautiously I approached, keeping my eyes upon the pretty little animal, and just as I was about to let fly my shaft, I heard a hissing noise at my feet. There lay a horrid snake, coiled and ready to spring! Forgetful that I was a warrior, I gave a loud scream and started backward; but soon recollecting myself, looked down with shame, although no one was near. However, I retreated to the inclined trunk of a fallen tree, and there, as I have often been told, was overheard soliloquizing in the following words: "I wonder if a snake can climb a tree!"

I remember on this occasion of our last sugar bush in Minnesota, that I stood one day outside of our hut and watched the approach of a visitor—a bent old man, his hair almost white, and carrying on his back a large bundle of red willow, or kinnikinick, which the Indians use for smoking. He threw down his load at the door and thus saluted us: "You have indeed perfect weather for sugar-making."

CHARLES A. EASTMAN

It was my great-grandfather, Cloud Man, whose original village was on the shores of Lakes Calhoun and Harriet, now in the suburbs of the city of Minneapolis. He was the first Sioux chief to welcome the Protestant missionaries among his people, and a well-known character in those pioneer days. He brought us word that some of the peaceful sugar-makers near us on the river had been attacked and murdered by roving Ojibways. This news disturbed us not a little, for we realized that we too might become the victims of an Ojibway war party. Therefore we all felt some uneasiness from this time until we returned heavy laden to our village.

V. A Midsummer Feast

IT WAS MIDSUMMER. EVERYTHING THAT the Santee Sioux had undertaken during the year had been unusually successful. The spring fur-hunters had been fortunate, and the heavy winter had proved productive of much maple sugar. The women's patches of maize and potatoes were already sufficiently advanced to use. The Wahpetonwan band of Sioux, the "Dwellers among the Leaves," were fully awakened to the fact that it was almost time for the midsummer festivities of the old, wild days.

The invitations were bundles of tobacco, and acceptances were sent back from the various bands—the "Light Lodges", "Dwellers back from the River," and many others, in similar fashion. Blue Earth, chief of the "Dwellers among the Leaves," was the host.

There were to be many different kinds of athletic games; indeed, the festival was something like a State fair, in that there were many side shows and competitive events. For instance, supposing that (Miss) White Rabbit should desire to give a "maidens' feast," she would employ a crier to go among the different bands announcing the fact in a sing-song manner:

"Miss White Rabbit will receive her maiden friends today at noon, inside of the circular encampment of the Kaposia band."

Again, should (Mr.) Sleepy Eye wish to have his child's ears pierced publicly, he would have to give away a great deal of savage wealth—namely, otter, bear and beaver skins and ponies—or the child would not be considered as belonging to a family in good standing.

But the one all-important event of the occasion was the lacrosse game, for which it had been customary to select those two bands which could boast the greater number of fast runners.

The Wahpetonwan village on the banks of the Minnesota river was alive with the newly-arrived guests and the preparations for the coming event. Meat of wild game had been put away with much care during the previous fall in anticipation of this feast. There was wild rice and the choicest of dried venison that had been kept all winter, as well as freshly dug turnips, ripe berries and an abundance of fresh meat.

Along the edge of the woods the teepees were pitched in groups or semi-circles, each band distinct from the others. The teepee of Mankato or Blue Earth was pitched in a conspicuous spot. Just over the entrance was painted in red and yellow a picture of a pipe, and directly opposite this the rising sun. The painting was symbolic of welcome and good will to men under the bright sun.

A meeting was held to appoint some "medicine man" to make the balls that were to be used in the lacrosse contest; and presently the herald announced that this honor had been conferred upon old Chankpee-yuhah, or "Keeps the Club," while every other man of his profession was disappointed. He was a powerful man physically, who had apparently won the confidence of the people by his fine personal appearance and by working upon superstitious minds.

Towards evening he appeared in the circle, leading by the hand a boy about four years old. Closely the little fellow observed every motion of the man; nothing escaped his vigilant black eyes, which seemed constantly to grow brighter and larger, while his exuberant glossy black hair was plaited and wound around his head like that of a Celestial. He wore a bit of swan's down in each ear, which formed a striking contrast with the child's complexion. Further than this, the boy was painted according to the fashion of the age. He held in his hands a miniature bow and arrows.

The medicine man drew himself up in an admirable attitude, and proceeded to make his short speech:

"Wahpetonwans, you boast that you run down the elk; you can outrun the Ojibways. Before you all, I dedicate to you this red ball. Kaposias, you claim that no one has a lighter foot than you; you declare that you can endure running a whole day without water. To you I dedicate this black ball. Either you or the Leaf-Dwellers will have to drop your eyes and bow your head when the game is over. I wish to announce that if the Wahpetonwans should win, this little warrior shall bear the name Ohiyesa (winner) through life; but if the Light Lodges should win, let the name be given to any child appointed by them."

The ground selected for the great final game was on a narrow strip of land between a lake and the river. It was about three quarters of a mile long and a quarter of a mile in width. The spectators had already ranged themselves all along the two sides, as well as at the two ends, which were somewhat higher than the middle. The soldiers appointed to keep order furnished much of the entertainment of the day. They painted artistically and tastefully, according to the Indian fashion, not only their bodies but also their ponies and clubs. They were so strict in enforcing the laws that no one could venture with safety within a few feet of the limits of the field.

Now all of the minor events and feasts, occupying several days' time, had been observed. Heralds on ponies' backs announced that all who intended to participate in the final game were requested to repair to the ground; also that if any one bore a grudge against another, he was implored to forget his ill-feeling until the contest should be over.

The most powerful men were stationed at the half-way ground, while the fast runners were assigned to the back. It was an impressive spectacle—a fine collection of agile forms, almost stripped of garments and painted in wild imitation of the rainbow and sunset sky on human canvas. Some had undertaken to depict the Milky Way across their tawny bodies, and one or two made a bold attempt to reproduce the lightning. Others contented themselves with painting the figure of some fleet animal or swift bird on their muscular chests.

The coiffure of the Sioux lacrosse player has often been unconsciously imitated by the fashionable hair-dressers of modern times. Some banged and singed their hair; others did a little more by adding powder. The Grecian knot was located on the wrong side of the head, being tied tightly over the forehead. A great many simply brushed back their long locks and tied them with a strip of otter skin.

At the middle of the ground were stationed four immense men, magnificently formed. A fifth approached this group, paused a moment, and then threw his head back, gazed up into the sky in the manner of a cock and gave a smooth, clear operatic tone. Instantly the little black ball went up between the two middle rushers, in the midst of yells, cheers and war-whoops. Both men endeavored to catch it in the air; but alas! each interfered with the other; then the guards on each side rushed upon them. For a time, a hundred lacrosse sticks vied with each other, and the wriggling human flesh and paint were all one could see through the cloud of dust. Suddenly there shot swiftly through the air toward the south, toward the Kaposias' goal, the ball. There was a general cheer from their adherents, which echoed back from the white cliff on the opposite side of the Minnesota.

As the ball flew through the air, two adversaries were ready to receive it. The Kaposia quickly met the ball, but failed to catch it in his netted bag, for the other had swung his up like a flash. Thus it struck the ground, but had no opportunity to bound up when a Wahpeton pounced upon it like a cat and slipped out of the grasp of his opponents. A mighty cheer thundered through the air.

The warrior who had undertaken to pilot the little sphere was risking much, for he must dodge a host of Kaposias before he could gain any ground. He was alert and agile; now springing like a panther, now leaping like a deer over a stooping opponent who tried to seize him around the waist. Every opposing player was upon his heels, while those of his own side did all in their power to clear the way for him. But it was all in vain. He only gained fifty paces.

Thus the game went. First one side, then the other would gain an advantage, and then it was lost, until the herald proclaimed that it was time to change the ball. No victory was in sight for either side.

After a few minutes' rest, the game was resumed. The red ball was now tossed in the air in the usual way. No sooner had it descended than one of the rushers caught it and away it went northward; again it was fortunate, for it was advanced by one of the same side. The scene was now one of the wildest excitement and confusion. At last, the northward flight of the ball was checked for a moment and a desperate struggle ensued. Cheers and war-whoops became general, such as were never equaled in any concourse of savages, and possibly nowhere except at a college game of football.

The ball had not been allowed to come to the surface since it reached this point, for there were more than a hundred men who scrambled for it. Suddenly a warrior shot out of the throng like the ball itself! Then some of the players shouted: "Look out for Antelope! Look out for Antelope!" But it was too late. The little sphere had already nestled into Antelope's palm and that fleetest of Wahpetons had thrown down his lacrosse stick and set a determined eye upon the northern goal.

Such a speed! He had cleared almost all the opponents' guards— there were but two more. These were exceptional runners of the Kaposias. As he approached them in his almost irresistible speed, every savage heart thumped louder in the Indian's dusky bosom. In another moment there would be a defeat for the Kaposias or a prolongation of the game. The two men, with a determined look approached their foe like two panthers prepared to spring; yet he neither slackened his speed nor deviated from his course. A crash—a mighty shout!—the two Kaposias collided, and the swift Antelope had won the laurels!

The turmoil and commotion at the victors' camp were indescribable. A few beats of a drum were heard, after which the criers hurried along the lines, announcing the last act to be performed at the camp of the "Leaf Dwellers."

The day had been a perfect one. Every event had been a success; and, as a matter of course, the old people were happy, for they largely profited by these occasions. Within the circle formed by the general assembly sat in a group the members of the common council. Blue Earth arose, and in a few appropriate and courteous remarks assured his guests that it was not selfishness that led his braves to carry off the honors of the last event, but that this was a friendly contest in which each band must assert its prowess. In memory of this victory, the boy would now receive his name. A loud "Ho-o-o" of approbation reverberated from the edge of the forest upon the Minnesota's bank.

Half frightened, the little fellow was now brought into the circle, looking very much as if he were about to be executed. Cheer after cheer went up for the awe-stricken boy. Chankpee-yuhah, the medicine man, proceeded to confer the name.

"Ohiyesa (or Winner) shall be thy name henceforth. Be brave, be patient and thou shalt always win! Thy name is Ohivesa."

II

An Indian Boy's Training

It is commonly supposed that there is no systematic education of their children among the aborigines of this country. Nothing could be farther from the truth. All the customs of this primitive people were held to be divinely instituted, and those in connection with the training of children were scrupulously adhered to and transmitted from one generation to another.

The expectant parents conjointly bent all their efforts to the task of giving the new-comer the best they could gather from a long line of ancestors. A pregnant Indian woman would often choose one of the greatest characters of her family and tribe as a model for her child. This hero was daily called to mind. She would gather from tradition all of his noted deeds and daring exploits, rehearsing them to herself when alone. In order that the impression might be more distinct, she avoided company. She isolated herself as much as possible, and wandered in solitude, not thoughtlessly, but with an eye to the impress given by grand and beautiful scenery.

The Indians believed, also, that certain kinds of animals would confer peculiar gifts upon the unborn, while others would leave so strong an adverse impression that the child might become a monstrosity. A case of hare-lip was commonly attributed to the rabbit. It was said that a rabbit had charmed the mother and given to the babe its own features. Even the meat of certain animals was denied the pregnant woman, because it was supposed to influence the disposition or features of the child.

Scarcely was the embryo warrior ushered into the world, when he was met by lullabies that speak of wonderful exploits in hunting and war. Those ideas which so fully occupied his mother's mind before his birth are now put into words by all about the child, who is as yet quite unresponsive to their appeals to his honor and ambition. He is called the future defender of his people, whose lives may depend upon his courage and skill. If the child is a girl, she is at once addressed as the future mother of a noble race.

In hunting songs, the leading animals are introduced; they come to the boy to offer their bodies for the sustenance of his tribe. The animals are regarded as his friends, and spoken of almost as tribes of people, or as his cousins, grandfathers and grandmothers. The songs of wooing, adapted as lullabies, were equally imaginative, and the suitors were often animals personified, while pretty maidens were represented by the mink and the doe.

Very early, the Indian boy assumed the task of preserving and transmitting the legends of his ancestors and his race. Almost every evening a myth, or a true story of some deed done in the past, was narrated by one of the parents or grandparents, while the boy listened with parted lips and glistening eyes. On the following evening, he was usually required to repeat it. If he was not an apt scholar, he struggled long with his task; but, as a rule, the Indian boy is a good listener and has a good memory, so that the stories were tolerably well mastered. The household became his audience, by which he was alternately criticized and applauded.

This sort of teaching at once enlightens the boy's mind and stimulates his ambition. His conception of his own future career becomes a vivid and irresistible force. Whatever there is for him to learn must be learned; whatever qualifications are necessary to a truly great man he must seek at any expense of danger and hardship. Such was the feeling of the imaginative and brave young Indian. It became apparent to him in early life that he must accustom himself to rove alone and not to fear or dislike the impression of solitude.

It seems to be a popular idea that all the characteristic skill of the Indian is instinctive and hereditary. This is a mistake. All the stoicism and patience of the Indian are acquired traits, and continual practice alone makes him master of the art of wood-craft. Physical training and dieting were not neglected. I remember that I was not allowed to have beef soup or any warm drink. The soup was for the old men. General rules for the young were never to take their food very hot, nor to drink much water.

My uncle, who educated me up to the age of fifteen years, was a strict disciplinarian and a good teacher. When I left the teepee in the morning, he would say: "Hakadah, look closely to everything you see"; and at evening, on my return, he used often to catechize me for an hour or so.

"On which side of the trees is the lighter-colored bark? On which side do they have most regular branches?"

It was his custom to let me name all the new birds that I had seen during the day. I would name them according to the color or the shape of the bill or their song or the appearance and locality of the nest—in fact, anything about the bird that impressed me as characteristic. I made many ridiculous errors, I must admit. He then usually informed me of the correct name. Occasionally I made a hit and this he would warmly commend.

He went much deeper into this science when I was a little older, that is, about the age of eight or nine years. He would say, for instance:

"How do you know that there are fish in yonder lake?"

"Because they jump out of the water for flies at mid-day."

He would smile at my prompt but superficial reply.

"What do you think of the little pebbles grouped together under the shallow water? and what made the pretty curved marks in the sandy bottom and the little sand-banks? Where do you find the fish-eating birds? Have the inlet and the outlet of a lake anything to do with the question?"

He did not expect a correct reply at once to all the voluminous questions that he put to me on these occasions, but he meant to make me observant and a good student of nature.

"Hakadah," he would say to me, "you ought to follow the example of the shunktokecha (wolf). Even when he is surprised and runs for his life, he will pause to take one more look at you before he enters his final retreat. So you must take a second look at everything you see.

"It is better to view animals unobserved. I have been a witness to their courtships and their quarrels and have learned many of their secrets in this way. I was once the unseen spectator of a thrilling battle between a pair of grizzly bears and three buffaloes—a rash act for the bears, for it was in the moon of strawberries, when the buffaloes sharpen and polish their horns for bloody contests among themselves.

"I advise you, my boy, never to approach a grizzly's den from the front, but to steal up behind and throw your blanket or a stone in front of the hole. He does not usually rush for it, but first puts his head out and listens and then comes out very indifferently and sits on his haunches on the mound in front of the hole before he makes any attack. While he is exposing himself in this fashion, aim at his heart. Always be as cool as the animal himself." Thus he armed me against the cunning of savage beasts by teaching me how to outwit them.

"In hunting," he would resume, "you will be guided by the habits of the animal you seek. Remember that a moose stays in swampy or low land or between high mountains near a spring or lake, for thirty to sixty days at a time. Most large game moves about continually, except the doe in the spring; it is then a very easy matter to find her with the fawn. Conceal yourself in a convenient place as soon as you observe any signs of the presence of either, and then call with your birchen doe-caller.

"Whichever one hears you first will soon appear in your neighborhood. But you must be very watchful, or you may be made a fawn of by a large wild-cat. They understand the characteristic call of the doe perfectly well.

"When you have any difficulty with a bear or a wild-cat—that is, if the creature shows signs of attacking you—you must make him fully understand that you have seen him and are aware of his intentions. If you are not well equipped for a pitched battle, the only way to make him retreat is to take a long sharp-pointed pole for a spear and rush toward him. No wild beast will face this unless he is cornered and already wounded. These fierce beasts are generally afraid of the common weapon of the larger animals—the horns, and if these are very long and sharp, they dare not risk an open fight.

"There is one exception to this rule—the grey wolf will attack fiercely when very hungry. But their courage depends upon their numbers; in this they are like white men. One wolf or two will never attack a man. They will stampede a herd of buffaloes in order to get at the calves; they will rush upon a herd of antelopes, for these are helpless; but they are always careful about attacking man."

Of this nature were the instructions of my uncle, who was widely known at that time as among the greatest hunters of his tribe.

All boys were expected to endure hardship without complaint. In savage warfare, a young man must, of course, be an athlete and used to undergoing all sorts of privations. He must be able to go without food and water for two or three days without displaying any weakness, or to run for a day and a night without any rest. He must be able to traverse a pathless and wild country without losing his way either in the day or night time. He cannot refuse to do any of these things if he aspires to be a warrior.

Sometimes my uncle would waken me very early in the morning and challenge me to fast with him all day. I had to accept the challenge. We blackened our faces with charcoal, so that every boy in the village would know that I was fasting for the day. Then the little tempters would make my life a misery until the merciful sun hid behind the western hills.

I can scarcely recall the time when my stern teacher began to give sudden war-whoops over my head in the morning while I was sound asleep. He expected me to leap up with perfect presence of mind, always ready to grasp a weapon of some sort and to give a shrill whoop in reply. If I was sleepy or startled and hardly knew what I was about, he would ridicule me and say that I need never expect to sell my scalp dear. Often he would vary these tactics by shooting off his gun just outside of the lodge while I was yet asleep, at the same time giving blood-curdling yells. After a time I became used to this.

When Indians went upon the war-path, it was their custom to try the new warriors thoroughly before coming to an engagement. For instance, when they were near a hostile camp, they would select the novices to go after the water and make them do all sorts of things to prove their courage. In accordance with this idea, my uncle used to send me off after water when we camped after dark in a strange place. Perhaps the country was full of wild beasts, and, for aught I knew, there might be scouts from hostile bands of Indians lurking in that very neighborhood.

Yet I never objected, for that would show cowardice. I picked my way through the woods, dipped my pail in the water and hurried back, always careful to make as little noise as a cat. Being only a boy, my heart would leap at every crackling of a dry twig or distant hooting of an owl, until, at last, I reached our teepee. Then my uncle would perhaps say: "Ah, Hakadah, you are a thorough warrior," empty out the precious contents of the pail, and order me to go a second time.

Imagine how I felt! But I wished to be a brave man as much as a white boy desires to be a great lawyer or even President of the United States. Silently I would take the pail and endeavor to retrace my footsteps in the dark.

With all this, our manners and morals were not neglected. I was made to respect the adults and especially the aged. I was not allowed to join in their discussions, nor even to speak in their presence, unless requested to do so. Indian etiquette was very strict, and among the requirements was that of avoiding the direct address. A term of relationship or some title of courtesy was commonly used instead of the personal name by those who wished to show respect. We were taught generosity to the poor and reverence for the "Great Mystery." Religion was the basis of all Indian training.

I recall to the present day some of the kind warnings and reproofs that my good grandmother was wont to give me. "Be strong of heart—

be patient!" she used to say. She told me of a young chief who was noted for his uncontrollable temper. While in one of his rages he attempted to kill a woman, for which he was slain by his own band and left unburied as a mark of disgrace—his body was simply covered with green grass. If I ever lost my temper, she would say:

"Hakadah, control yourself, or you will be like that young man I told you of, and lie under a green blanket!"

In the old days, no young man was allowed to use tobacco in any form until he had become an acknowledged warrior and had achieved a record. If a youth should seek a wife before he had reached the age of twenty-two or twenty-three, and been recognized as a brave man, he was sneered at and considered an ill-bred Indian. He must also be a skillful hunter. An Indian cannot be a good husband unless he brings home plenty of game.

These precepts were in the line of our training for the wild life.

III

My Plays and Playmates

I. Games and Sports

The Indian boy was a prince of the wilderness. He had but very little work to do during the period of his boyhood. His principal occupation was the practice of a few simple arts in warfare and the chase. Aside from this, he was master of his time.

Whatever was required of us boys was quickly performed: then the field was clear for our games and plays. There was always keen competition among us. We felt very much as our fathers did in hunting and war—each one strove to excel all the others.

It is true that our savage life was a precarious one, and full of dreadful catastrophes; however, this never prevented us from enjoying our sports to the fullest extent. As we left our teepees in the morning, we were never sure that our scalps would not dangle from a pole in the afternoon! It was an uncertain life, to be sure. Yet we observed that the fawns skipped and played happily while the gray wolves might be peeping forth from behind the hills, ready to tear them limb from limb.

Our sports were molded by the life and customs of our people; indeed, we practiced only what we expected to do when grown. Our games were feats with the bow and arrow, foot and pony races, wrestling, swimming and imitation of the customs and habits of our fathers. We had sham fights with mud balls and willow wands; we played lacrosse, made war upon bees, shot winter arrows (which were used only in that season), and coasted upon the ribs of animals and buffalo robes.

No sooner did the boys get together than, as a usual thing, they divided into squads and chose sides; then a leading arrow was shot at random into the air. Before it fell to the ground a volley from the bows of the participants followed. Each player was quick to note the direction and speed of the leading arrow and he tried to send his own at the same speed and at an equal height, so that when it fell it would be closer to the first than any of the others.

It was considered out of place to shoot by first sighting the object aimed at. This was usually impracticable in actual life, because the object was almost always in motion, while the hunter himself was often upon the back of a pony at full gallop. Therefore, it was the off-hand shot that the Indian boy sought to master. There was another game with arrows that was characterized by gambling, and was generally confined to the men.

The races were an every-day occurrence. At noon the boys were usually gathered by some pleasant sheet of water and as soon as the ponies were watered, they were allowed to graze for an hour or two, while the boys stripped for their noonday sports. A boy might say to some other whom he considered his equal:

"I can't run; but I will challenge you to fifty paces."

A former hero, when beaten, would often explain his defeat by saying: "I drank too much water."

Boys of all ages were paired for a "spin," and the little red men cheered on their favorites with spirit.

As soon as this was ended, the pony races followed. All the speedy ponies were picked out and riders chosen. If a boy declined to ride, there would be shouts of derision.

Last of all came the swimming. A little urchin would hang to his pony's long tail, while the latter, with only his head above water, glided sportively along. Finally the animals were driven into a fine field of grass and we turned our attention to other games.

Lacrosse was an older game and was confined entirely to the Sisseton and Santee Sioux. Shinny, such as is enjoyed by white boys on the ice, is still played on the open prairie by the western Sioux. The "moccasin game," although sometimes played by the boys, was intended mainly for adults.

The "mud-and-willow" fight was rather a severe and dangerous sport. A lump of soft clay was stuck on the end of a limber and springy willow wand and thrown as boys throw apples from sticks, with considerable force. When there were fifty or a hundred players on each side, the battle became warm; but anything to arouse the bravery of Indian boys seemed to them a good and wholesome diversion.

Wrestling was largely indulged in by us all. It may seem odd,, but wrestling was done by a great many boys at once—from ten to any number on a side. It was really a battle, in which each one chose his opponent. The rule was that if a boy sat down, he was let alone, but as long as he remained standing within the field, he was open to an attack. No one struck with the hand, but all manner of tripping with legs and feet and butting with the knees was allowed. Altogether it was an exhausting pastime—fully equal to the American game of football and only the young athlete could really enjoy it.

One of our most curious sports was a war upon the nests of wild bees. We imagined ourselves about to make an attack upon the Ojibways or some tribal foe. We all painted and stole cautiously upon the nest; then, with a rush and warwhoop, sprang upon the object of our attack and endeavored to destroy it. But it seemed that the bees were always on the alert and never entirely surprised, for they always raised quite as many scalps as did their bold assailants! After the onslaught upon the nest was ended, we usually followed it by a pretended scalp dance.

On the occasion of my first experience in this mode of warfare, there were two other little boys who were also novices. One of them particularly was really too young to indulge in an exploit of that kind. As it was the custom of our people, when they killed or wounded an enemy on the battle field, to announce the act in a loud voice, we did the same. My friend, Little Wound (as I will call him, for I do not remember his name), being quite small, was unable to reach the nest until it had been well trampled upon and broken and the insects had made a counter charge with such vigor as to repulse and scatter our numbers in every direction. However, he evidently did not want to retreat without any honors; so he bravely jumped upon the nest and yelled:

"I, the brave Little Wound, today kill the only fierce enemy!"

Scarcely were the last words uttered when he screamed as if stabbed to the heart. One of his older companions shouted:

"Dive into the water! Run! Dive into the water!" for there was a lake near by. This advice he obeyed.

When we had reassembled and were indulging in our mimic dance, Little Wound was not allowed to dance. He was considered not to be in existence—he had been killed by our enemies, the Bee tribe. Poor little fellow! His swollen face was sad and ashamed as he sat on a fallen log and watched the dance. Although he might well have styled himself one of the noble dead who had died for their country, yet he was not unmindful that he had screamed, and this weakness would be apt to recur to him many times in the future.

We had some quiet plays which we alternated with the more severe and warlike ones. Among them were throwing wands and snow-arrows. In the winter we coasted much. We had no "double-rippers" or toboggans, but six or seven of the long ribs of a buffalo, fastened together at the larger end, answered all practical purposes. Sometimes a strip of bass-wood bark, four feet long and about six inches wide, was used with considerable skill. We stood on one end and held the other, using the slippery inside of the bark for the outside, and thus coasting down long hills with remarkable speed.

The spinning of tops was one of the all-absorbing winter sports. We made our tops heartshaped of wood, horn or bone. We whipped them with a long thong of buckskin. The handle was a stick about a foot long and sometimes we whittled the stick to make it spoon-shaped at one end.

We played games with these tops—two to fifty boys at one time. Each whips his top until it hums; then one takes the lead and the rest follow in a sort of obstacle race. The top must spin all the way through. There were bars of snow over which we must pilot our top in the spoon end of our whip; then again we would toss it in the air on to another open spot of ice or smooth snowcrust from twenty to fifty paces away. The top that holds out the longest is the winner.

Sometimes we played "medicine dance." This, to us, was almost what "playing church" is among white children, but our people seemed to think it an act of irreverence to imitate these dances, therefore performances of this kind were always enjoyed in secret. We used to observe all the important ceremonies and it required something of an actor to reproduce the dramatic features of the dance. The real dances occupied a day and a night, and the program was long and varied, so that it was not easy to execute all the details perfectly; but the Indian children are born imitators.

The boys built an arbor of pine boughs in some out-of-the-way place and at one end of it was a rude lodge. This was the medicine lodge or headquarters. All the initiates were there. At the further end or entrance were the door-keepers or soldiers, as we called them. The members of each lodge entered in a body, standing in single file and facing the headquarters. Each stretched out his right hand and a prayer was offered by the leader, after which they took the places assigned to them.

When the preliminaries had been completed, our leader sounded the big drum and we all said "A-ho-ho-ho!" as a sort of amen. Then the choir began their song and whenever they ended a verse, we all said again "A-ho-ho-ho!" At last they struck up the chorus and we all got upon our feet and began to dance, by simply lifting up one foot and then the other, with a slight swing to the body.

Each boy was representing or imitating some one of the medicine men. We painted and decorated ourselves just as they did and carried bird or squirrel skins, or occasionally live birds and chipmunks as our medicine bags and small white shells or pebbles for medicine charms.

Then the persons to be initiated were brought in and seated, with much ceremony, upon a blanket or buffalo robe. Directly in front of them the ground was levelled smooth and here we laid an old pipe filled with dried leaves for tobacco. Around it we placed the variously colored feathers of the birds we had killed, and cedar and sweetgrass we burned for incense.

Finally those of us who had been selected to perform this ceremony stretched out our arms at full length, holding the sacred medicine bags and aiming them at the new members. After swinging them four times, we shot them suddenly forward, but did not let go. The novices then fell forward on their faces as if dead. Quickly a chorus was struck up and we all joined in a lively dance around the supposed bodies. The girls covered them up with their blankets, thus burying the dead. At last we resurrected them with our charms and led them to their places among the audience. Then came the last general dance and the final feast.

I was often selected as choir-master on these occasions, for I had happened to learn many of the medicine songs and was quite an apt mimic. My grandmother, who was a noted medicine woman of the Turtle lodge, on hearing of these sacrilegious acts (as she called them) warned me that if any of the medicine men should discover them, they would punish me terribly by shriveling my limbs with slow disease.

Occasionally, we also played "white man." Our knowledge of the pale-face was limited, but we had learned that he brought goods whenever he came and that our people exchanged furs for his merchandise. We also knew that his complexion was pale, that he had short hair on his head and long hair on his face and that he wore coat, trousers, and hat, and did not patronize blankets in the daytime. This was the picture we had formed of the white man.

So we painted two or three of our number with white clay and put on them birchen hats which we sewed up for the occasion; fastened a piece of fur to their chins for a beard and altered their costumes as much as lay within our power. The white of the birch-bark was made to answer for their white shirts. Their merchandise consisted of sand for sugar, wild beans for coffee, dried leaves for tea, pulverized earth for gun-powder, pebbles for bullets and clear water for the dangerous "spirit water." We traded for these goods with skins of squirrels, rabbits and small birds.

When we played "hunting buffalo" we would send a few good runners off on the open prairie with a supply of meat; then start a few equally swift boys to chase them and capture the food. Once we were engaged in this sport when a real hunt by the men was in progress; yet we did not realize that it was so near until, in the midst of our play, we saw an immense buffalo coming at full speed directly toward us. Our mimic buffalo hunt turned into a very real buffalo scare. Fortunately, we were near the edge of the woods and we soon disappeared among the leaves like a covey of young prairie-chickens and some hid in the bushes while others took refuge in tall trees.

We loved to play in the water. When we had no ponies, we often had swimming matches of our own and sometimes made rafts with which we crossed lakes and rivers. It was a common thing to "duck" a young or timid boy or to carry him into deep water to struggle as best he might.

I remember a perilous ride with a companion on an unmanageable log, when we were both less than seven years old. The older boys had put us on this uncertain bark and pushed us out into the swift current of the river. I cannot speak for my comrade in distress, but I can say now that I would rather ride on a swift bronco any day than try to stay on and steady a short log in a river. I never knew how we managed to prevent a shipwreck on that voyage and to reach the shore.

We had many curious wild pets. There were young foxes, bears, wolves, raccoons, fawns, buffalo calves and birds of all kinds, tamed by various boys. My pets were different at different times, but I particularly remember one. I once had a grizzly bear for a pet and so far as he and I were concerned, our relations were charming and very close. But I hardly know whether he made more enemies for me or I for him. It was his habit to treat every boy unmercifully who injured me. He was despised for his conduct in my interest and I was hated on account of his interference.

II. My Playmates

CHATANNA WAS THE BROTHER WITH whom I passed much of my early childhood. From the time that I was old enough to play with boys, this brother was my close companion. He was a handsome boy, and affectionate comrade. We played together, slept together and ate together; and as Chatanna was three years the older, I naturally looked up to him as to a superior.

Oesedah was a beautiful little character. She was my cousin, and four years younger than myself. Perhaps none of my early playmates are more vividly remembered than is this little maiden.

The name given her by a noted medicine-man was Makah-oesetopah-win. It means The-four-corners-of-the-earth. As she was rather small, the abbreviation with a diminutive termination was considered more appropriate, hence Oesedah became her common name.

Although she had a very good mother, Uncheedah was her efficient teacher and chaperon Such knowledge as my grandmother deemed suitable to a maiden was duly impressed upon her susceptible mind. When I was not in the woods with Chatanna, Oesedah was my companion at home; and when I returned from my play at evening, she would have a hundred questions ready for me to answer. Some of these were questions concerning our every-day life, and others were more difficult problems which had suddenly dawned upon her active little mind. Whatever had occurred to interest her during the day was immediately repeated for my benefit.

There were certain questions upon which Oesedah held me to be authority, and asked with the hope of increasing her little store of knowledge. I have often heard her declare to her girl companions: "I know it is true; Ohiyesa said so!" Uncheedah was partly responsible for this, for when any questions came up which lay within the sphere of man's observation, she would say:

"Ohiyesa ought to know that: he is a man—I am not! You had better ask him."

The truth was that she had herself explained to me many of the subjects under discussion.

I was occasionally referred to little Oesedah in the same manner, and I always accepted her childish elucidations of any matter upon which I had been advised to consult her, because I knew the source of her wisdom. In this simple way we were made to be teachers of one another.

Very often we discussed some topic before our common instructor, or answered her questions together, in order to show which had the readier mind.

"To what tribe does the lizard belong?" inquired Uncheedah, upon one of these occasions.

"To the four-legged tribe," I shouted.

Oesedah, with her usual quickness, flashed out the answer:

"It belongs to the creeping tribe."

The Indians divided all animals into four general classes: 1st, those that walk upon four legs; 2nd, those that fly; 3rd, those that swim with fins; 4th, those that creep.

Of course I endeavored to support my assertion that the lizard belongs where I had placed it, be-. cause he has four distinct legs which propel him everywhere, on the ground or in the water. But my opponent claimed that the creature under dispute does not walk, but creeps. My strongest argument was that it had legs; but Oesedah insisted that its body touches the ground as it moves. As a last resort, I volunteered to go find one, and demonstrate the point in question.

The lizard having been brought, we smoothed off the ground and strewed ashes on it so that we could see the track. Then I raised the question: "What constitutes creeping, and what constitutes walking?"

Uncheedah was the judge, and she stated, without any hesitation, that an animal must stand clear of the ground on the support of its legs, and walk with the body above the legs, and not in contact with the ground, in order to be termed a walker; while a creeper is one that, regardless of its legs, if it has them, drags its body upon the ground. Upon hearing the judge's decision, I yielded at once to my opponent.

At another time, when I was engaged in a similar discussion with my brother Chatanna, Oesedah came to my rescue. Our grandmother had asked us:

"What bird shows most judgment in caring for its young?"

Chatanna at once exclaimed:

"The eagle!" but I held my peace for a moment, because I was confused—so many birds came into my mind at once. I finally declared:

"It is the oriole!"

Chatanna was asked to state all the evidence that he had in support of the eagle's good sense in rearing its young. He proceeded with an air of confidence:

"The eagle is the wisest of all birds. Its nest is made in the safest possible place, upon a high and inaccessible cliff. It provides its young with an abundance of fresh meat. They have the freshest of air. They are brought up under the spell of the grandest scenes, and inspired with lofty feelings and bravery. They see that all other beings live beneath them, and that they are the children of the King of Birds. A young eagle shows the spirit of a warrior while still in the nest.

"Being exposed to the inclemency of the weather the young eaglets are hardy. They are accustomed to hear the mutterings of the Thunder Bird and the sighings of the Great Mystery. Why, the little eagles cannot help being as noble as they are, because their parents selected for them so lofty and inspiring a home! How happy they must be when they find themselves above the clouds, and behold the zigzag flashes of lightning all about them! It must be nice to taste a piece of fresh meat up in their cool home, in the burning summer-time! Then when they drop down the bones of the game they feed upon, wolves and vultures gather beneath them, feeding upon their refuse. That alone would show them their chieftainship over all the other birds. Isn't that so, grandmother?" Thus triumphantly he concluded his argument.

I was staggered at first by the noble speech of Chatannna, but I soon recovered from its effects. The little Oesedah came to my aid by saying: "Wait until Ohiyesa tells of the loveliness of the beautiful Oriole's home!" This timely remark gave me courage and I began:

"My grandmother, who was it said that a mother who has a gentle and sweet voice will have children of a good disposition? I think the oriole is that kind of a parent. It provides both sunshine and shadow for its young. Its nest is suspended from the prettiest bough of the most graceful tree, where it is rocked by the gentle winds; and the one we found yesterday was beautifully lined with soft things, both deep and warm, so that the little featherless birdies cannot suffer from the cold and wet."

Here Chatanna interrupted me to exclaim: "That is just like the white people—who cares for them? The eagle teaches its young to be accustomed to hardships, like young warriors!"

Ohiyesa was provoked; he reproached his brother and appealed to the judge, saying that he had not finished yet.

"But you would not have lived, Chatanna, if you had been exposed like that when you were a baby! The oriole shows wisdom in providing for its children a good, comfortable home! A home upon a high rock would not be pleasant—it would be cold! We climbed a mountain once, and it was cold there; and who would care to stay in such a place when it storms? What wisdom is there in having a pile of rough sticks upon a bare rock, surrounded with ill-smelling bones of animals, for a home? Also, my uncle says that the eaglets seem always to be on the point of starvation. You have heard that whoever lives on game killed by some one else is compared to an eagle. Isn't that so, grandmother?

"The oriole suspends its nest from the lower side of a horizontal bough so that no enemy can approach it. It enjoys peace and beauty and safety."

Oesedah was at Ohiyesa's side during the discussion, and occasionally whispered into his ear. Uncheedah decided this time in favor of Ohiyesa.

We were once very short of provisions in the winter time. My uncle, our only means of support, was sick; and besides, we were separated from the rest of the tribe and in a region where there was little game of any kind. Oesedah had a pet squirrel, and as soon as we began to economize our food had given portions of her allowance to her pet.

At last we were reduced very much, and the prospect of obtaining anything soon being gloomy, my grandmother reluctantly suggested that the squirrel should be killed for food. Thereupon my little cousin cried, and said:

"Why cannot we all die alike wanting? The squirrel's life is as dear to him as ours to us," and clung to it. Fortunately, relief came in time to save her pet.

Oesedah lived with us for a portion of the year, and as there were no other girls in the family she played much alone, and had many imaginary companions. At one time there was a small willow tree which she visited regularly, holding long conversations, a part of which she would afterward repeat to me. She said the willow tree was her husband, whom some magic had compelled to take that form; but no grown person was ever allowed to share her secret.

When I was about eight years old I had for a playmate the adopted son of a Sioux, who was a white captive. This boy was quite a noted personage, although he was then only about ten or eleven years of age. When I first became acquainted with him we were on the upper Missouri river. I learned from him that he had been taken on the plains, and that both of his parents were killed.

He was at first sad and lonely, but soon found plenty of consolation in his new home. The name of his adopted father was "Keeps-the-Spotted-Ponies." He was known to have an unusual number of the pretty calico ponies; indeed, he had a passion for accumulating property in the shape of ponies, painted tents, decorated saddles and all sorts of finery. He had lost his only son; but the little pale-face became the adopted brother of two handsome young women, his daughters. This made him quite popular among the young warriors. He was not slow to adopt the Indian customs, and he acquired the Sioux language in a short time.

I well remember hearing of his first experience of war. He was not more than sixteen when he joined a war-party against the Gros-Ventres and Mandans. My uncle reported that he was very brave until he was wounded in the ankle; then he begged with tears to be taken back to a safe place. Fortunately for him, his adopted father came to the rescue, and saved him at the risk of his own life. He was called the "pale-face Indian." His hair grew very long and he lavished paint on his face and hair so that no one might suspect that he was a white man.

One day this boy was playing a gambling game with one of the Sioux warriors. He was an expert gambler, and won everything from the Indian. At a certain point a dispute arose. The Indian was very angry, for he discovered that his fellow-player had deliberately cheated him. The Indians were strictly honest in those days, even in their gambling.

The boy declared that he had merely performed a trick for the benefit of his friend, but it nearly cost him his life. The indignant warrior had already drawn his bow-string with the intention of shooting the captive, but a third person intervened and saved the boy's life. He at once explained his trick; and in order to show himself an honorable gambler, gave back all the articles that he had won from his opponent. In the midst of the confusion, old "Keeps-the-Spotted-Ponies" came rushing through the crowd in a state of great excitement. He thought his pale-face son had been killed. When he saw how matters stood, he gave the aggrieved warrior a pony, "in order," as he said, "that there may be no shadow between him and my son."

One spring my uncle took Chatanna to the Canadian trading-post on the Assiniboine river, where he went to trade off his furs for ammunition and other commodities. When he came back, my brother was not with him!

At first my fears were even worse than the reality. The facts were these: A Canadian with whom my uncle had traded much had six daughters and no son; and when he saw this handsome and intelligent little fellow, he at once offered to adopt him.

"I have no boy in my family," said he, "and I will deal with him as with a son. I am always in these regions trading; so you can see him two or three times in a year."

He further assured my uncle that the possession of the boy would greatly strengthen their friendship. The matter was finally agreed upon. At first Chatanna was unwilling, but as we were taught to follow the advice of our parents and guardians, he was obliged to yield.

This was a severe blow to me, and for a long time I could not be consoled. Uncheedah was fully in sympathy with my distress. She argued that the white man's education was not desirable for her boys; in fact, she urged her son so strongly to go back after Chatanna that he promised on his next visit to the post to bring him home again.

But the trader was a shrewd man. He immediately moved to another part of the country; and I never saw my Chatanna, the companion of my childhood, again! We learned afterward that he grew up and was married; but one day he lost his way in a blizzard and was frozen to death.

My little cousin and I went to school together in later years; but she could not endure the confinement of the school-room. Although apparently very happy, she suffered greatly from the change to an indoor life, as have many of our people, and died six months after our return to the United States.

III. The Boy Hunter

IT WILL BE NO EXAGGERATION to say that the life of the Indian hunter was a life of fascination. From the moment that he lost sight of his rude home in the midst of the forest, his untutored mind lost itself in the myriad beauties and forces of nature. Yet he never forgot his personal danger from some lurking foe or savage beast, however absorbing was his passion for the chase.

The Indian youth was a born hunter. Every motion, every step expressed an inborn dignity and, at the same time, a depth of native caution. His moccasined foot fell like the velvet paw of a cat— noiselessly; his glittering black eyes scanned every object that appeared within their view. Not a bird, not even a chipmunk, escaped their piercing glance.

I was scarcely over three years old when I stood one morning just outside our buffalo-skin teepee, with my little bow and arrows in my hand, and gazed up among the trees. Suddenly the instinct to chase and kill seized me powerfully. Just then a bird flew over my head and then another caught my eye, as it balanced itself upon a swaying bough.

Everything else was forgotten and in that moment I had taken my first step as a hunter.

There was almost as much difference between the Indian boys who were brought up on the open prairies and those of the woods, as between city and country boys. The hunting of the prairie boys was limited and their knowledge of natural history imperfect. They were, as a rule, good riders, but in all-round physical development much inferior to the red men of the forest.

Our hunting varied with the season of the year, and the nature of the country which was for the time our home. Our chief weapon was the bow and arrows, and perhaps, if we were lucky, a knife was possessed by some one in the crowd. In the olden times, knives and hatchets were made from bone and sharp stones.

For fire we used a flint with a spongy piece of dry wood and a stone to strike with. Another way of starting fire was for several of the boys to sit down in a circle and rub two pieces of dry, spongy wood together, one after another, until the wood took fire.

We hunted in company a great deal, though it was a common thing for a boy to set out for the woods quite alone, and he usually enjoyed himself fully as much. Our game consisted mainly of small birds, rabbits, squirrels and grouse. Fishing, too, occupied much of our time. We hardly ever passed a creek or a pond without searching for some signs of fish. When fish were present, we always managed to get some. Fish-lines were made of wild hemp, sinew or horse-hair. We either caught fish with lines, snared or speared them, or shot them with bow and arrows. In the fall we charmed them up to the surface by gently tickling them with a stick and quickly threw them out. We have sometimes dammed the brooks and driven the larger fish into a willow basket made for that purpose.

It was part of our hunting to find new and strange things in the woods. We examined the slightest sign of life; and if a bird had scratched the leaves off the ground, or a bear dragged up a root for his morning meal, we stopped to speculate on the time it was done. If we saw a large old tree with some scratches on its bark, we concluded that a bear or some raccoons must be living there. In that case we did not go any nearer than was necessary, but later reported the incident at home. An old deer-track would at once bring on a warm discussion as to whether it was the track of a buck or a doe. Generally, at noon, we met and compared our game, noting at the same time the peculiar characteristics of everything we had killed. It was not merely a hunt, for we combined with it the study of animal life. We also kept strict account of our game, and thus learned who were the best shots among the boys.

I am sorry to say that we were merciless toward the birds. We often took their eggs and their young ones. My brother Chatanna and I once had a disagreeable adventure while bird-hunting. We were accustomed to catch in our hands young ducks and geese during the summer, and while doing this we happened to find a crane's nest. Of course, we were delighted with our good luck. But, as it was already midsummer, the young cranes—two in number—were rather large and they were a little way from the nest; we also observed that the two old cranes were in a swampy place near by; but, as it was moulting-time, we did not suppose that they would venture on dry land. So we proceeded to chase the young birds; but they were fleet runners and it took us some time to come up with them.

Meanwhile, the parent birds had heard the cries of their little ones and come to their rescue. They were chasing us, while we followed the birds. It was really a perilous encounter! Our strong bows finally gained the victory in a hand-to-hand struggle with the angry cranes; but after that we hardly ever hunted a crane's nest. Almost all birds make some resistance when their eggs or young are taken, but they will seldom attack man fearlessly.

We used to climb large trees for birds of all kinds; but we never undertook to get young owls unless they were on the ground. The hooting owl especially is a dangerous bird to attack under these circumstances. I was once trying to catch a yellow-winged woodpecker in its nest when my arm became twisted and lodged in the deep hole so that I could not get it out without the aid of a knife; but we were a long way from home and my only companion was a deaf mute cousin of mine. I was about fifty feet up in the tree, in a very uncomfortable position, but I had to wait there for more than an hour before he brought me the knife with which I finally released myself.

Our devices for trapping small animals were rude, but they were often successful. For instance, we used to gather up a peck or so of large, sharp-pointed burrs and scatter them in the rabbit's furrow-like path. In the morning, we would find the little fellow sitting quietly in his tracks, unable to move, for the burrs stuck to his feet.

Another way of snaring rabbits and grouse was the following: We made nooses of twisted horsehair, which we tied very firmly to the top of a limber young tree, then bent the latter down to the track and fastened the whole with a slip-knot, after adjusting the noose. When the rabbit runs his head through the noose, he pulls the slip-knot and is quickly carried up by the spring of the young tree. This is a good plan, for the rabbit is out of harm's way as he swings high in the air.

Perhaps the most enjoyable of all was the chipmunk hunt. We killed these animals at any time of year, but the special time to hunt them was in March. After the first thaw, the chipmunks burrow a hole through the snow crust and make their first appearance for the season. Sometimes as many as fifty will come together and hold a social reunion. These gatherings occur early in the morning, from daybreak to about nine o'clock.

We boys learned this, among other secrets of nature, and got our blunt-headed arrows together in good season for the chipmunk expedition.

We generally went in groups of six to a dozen or fifteen, to see which would get the most. On the evening before, we selected several boys who could imitate the chipmunk's call with wild oatstraws and each of these provided himself with a supply of straws.

The crust will hold the boys nicely at this time of the year. Bright and early, they all come together at the appointed place, from which each group starts out in a different direction, agreeing to meet somewhere at a given position of the sun.

My first experience of this kind is still well remembered. It was a fine crisp March morning, and the sun had not yet shown himself among the distant tree-tops as we hurried along through the ghostly wood. Presently we arrived at a place where there were many signs of the animals. Then each of us selected a tree and took up his position behind it. The chipmunk caller sat upon a log as motionless as he could, and began to call.

Soon we heard the patter of little feet on the hard snow; then we saw the chipmunks approaching from all directions. Some stopped and ran experimentally up a tree or a log, as if uncertain of the exact direction of the call; others chased one another about.

In a few minutes, the chipmunk-caller was besieged with them. Some ran all over his person, others under him and still others ran up the tree against which he was sitting. Each boy remained immovable until their leader gave the signal; then a great shout arose, and the chipmunks in their flight all ran up the different trees.

Now the shooting-match began. The little creatures seemed to realize their hopeless position; they would try again and again to come down the trees and flee away from the deadly aim of the youthful hunters. But they were shot down very fast; and whenever several of them rushed toward the ground, the little red-skin hugged the tree and yelled frantically to scare them up again.

Each boy shoots always against the trunk of the tree, so that the arrow may bound back to him every time; otherwise, when he had shot away all of them, he would be helpless, and another, who had cleared his own tree, would come and take away his game, so there was warm competition. Sometimes a desperate chipmunk would jump from the top of the tree in order to escape, which was considered a joke on the boy who lost it and a triumph for the brave little animal. At last all were killed or gone, and then we went on to another place, keeping up the sport until the sun came out and the chipmunks refused to answer the call.

When we went out on the prairies we had a different and less lively kind of sport. We used to snare with horse-hair and bow-strings all the small ground animals, including the prairie-dog. We both snared and shot them. Once a little boy set a snare for one, and lay flat on the ground a little way from the hole, holding the end of the string. Presently he felt something move and pulled in a huge rattlesnake; and to this day, his name is "Caught-the-Rattlesnake." Very often a boy got a new name in some such manner. At another time, we were playing in the woods and found a fawn's track. We followed and caught it while asleep; but in the struggle to get away, it kicked one boy, who is still called "Kicked-by-the-Fawn."

It became a necessary part of our education to learn to prepare a meal while out hunting. It is a fact that most Indians will eat the liver and some other portions of large animals raw, but they do not eat fish or birds uncooked. Neither will they eat a frog, or an eel. On our boyish hunts, we often went on until we found ourselves a long way from our camp, when we would kindle a fire and roast a part of our game.

Generally we broiled our meat over the coals on a stick. We roasted some of it over the open fire. But the best way to cook fish and birds is in the ashes, under a big fire. We take the fish fresh from the creek or lake, have a good fire on the sand, dig in the sandy ashes and bury it deep. The same thing is done in case of a bird, only we wet the feathers first. When it is done, the scales or feathers and skin are stripped off whole, and the delicious meat retains all its juices and flavor. We pulled it off as we ate, leaving the bones undisturbed.

Our people had also a method of boiling without pots or kettles. A large piece of tripe was thoroughly washed and the ends tied, then suspended between four stakes driven into the ground and filled with cold water. The meat was then placed in this novel receptacle and boiled by means of the addition of red-hot stones.

Chatanna was a good hunter. He called the doe and fawn beautifully by using a thin leaf of birchbark between two flattened sticks. One morning we found the tracks of a doe and fawn who had passed within the hour, for the light dew was brushed from the grass.

"What shall we do?" I asked. "Shall we go back to the teepee and tell uncle to bring his gun?"

"No, no!" exclaimed Chatanna. "Did not our people kill deer and buffalo long ago without guns? We will entice her into this open space, and, while she stands bewildered, I can throw my lasso line over her head."

He had called only a few seconds when the fawn emerged from the thick woods and stood before us, prettier than a picture. Then I uttered the call, and she threw her tobacco-leaf-like ears toward me, while Chatanna threw his lasso. She gave one scream and launched forth into the air, almost throwing the boy hunter to the ground. Again and again she flung herself desperately into the air, but at last we led her to the nearest tree and tied her securely.

"Now," said he, "go and get our pets and see what they will do."

At that time he had a good-sized black bear partly tamed, while I had a young red fox and my faithful Ohitika or Brave. I untied Chagoo, the bear, and Wanahon, the fox, while Ohitika got up and welcomed me by wagging his tail in a dignified way.

"Come," I said, "all three of you. I think we have something you would all like to see."

They seemed to understand me, for Chagoo began to pull his rope with both paws, while Wanahon undertook the task of digging up by the roots the sapling to which I had tied him.

Before we got to the open spot, we already heard Ohitika's joyous bark, and the two wild pets began to run, and pulled me along through the underbrush. Chagoo soon assumed the utmost precaution and walked as if he had splinters in his soles, while Wanahon kept his nose down low and sneaked through the trees.

Out into the open glade we came, and there, before the three rogues, stood the little innocent fawn. She visibly trembled at the sight of the motley group. The two human rogues looked to her, I presume, just as bad as the other three. Chagoo regarded her with a mixture of curiosity and defiance, while Wanahon stood as if rooted to the ground, evidently planning how to get at her. But Ohitika (Brave), generous Ohitika, his occasional barking was only in jest. He did not care to touch the helpless thing.

Suddenly the fawn sprang high into the air and then dropped her pretty head on the ground.

"Ohiyesa, the fawn is dead," cried Chatanna. "I wanted to keep her."

"It is a shame;" I chimed in.

We five guilty ones came and stood around her helpless form. We all looked very sorry; even Chagoo's eyes showed repentance and regret. As for Ohitika, he gave two great sighs and then betook himself to a respectful distance. Chatanna had two big tears gradually swamping his long, black eye-lashes; and I thought it was time to hide my face, for I did not want him to look at me.

IV

Hakadah's First Offering

Hakadah, coowah!" was the sonorous call that came from a large teepee in the midst of the Indian encampment. In answer to the summons there emerged from the woods, which were only a few steps away, a boy, accompanied by a splendid black dog. There was little in the appearance of the little fellow to distinguish him from the other Sioux boys.

He hastened to the tent from which he had been summoned, carrying in his hands a bow and arrows gorgeously painted, while the small birds and squirrels that he had killed with these weapons dangled from his belt.

Within the tent sat two old women, one on each side of the fire. Uncheedah was the boy's grandmother, who had brought up the motherless child. Wahchewin was only a caller, but she had been invited to remain and assist in the first personal offering of Hakadah to the "Great Mystery."

This was a matter which had, for several days, pretty much monopolized Uncheedah's mind. It was her custom to see to this when each of her children attained the age of eight summers. They had all been celebrated as warriors and hunters among their tribe, and she had not hesitated to claim for herself a good share of the honors they had achieved, because she had brought them early to the notice of the "Great Mystery."

She believed that her influence had helped to regulate and develop the characters of her sons to the height of savage nobility and strength of manhood.

It had been whispered through the teepee village that Uncheedah intended to give a feast in honor of her grandchild's first sacrificial offering. This was mere speculation, however, for the clearsighted old woman had determined to keep this part of the matter secret until the offering should be completed, believing that the "Great Mystery" should be met in silence and dignity.

The boy came rushing into the lodge, followed by his dog Ohitika who was wagging his tail promiscuously, as if to say: "Master and I are really hunters!"

Hakadah breathlessly gave a descriptive narrative of the killing of each bird and squirrel as he pulled them off his belt and threw them before his grandmother.

"This blunt-headed arrow," said he, "actually had eyes this morning. Before the squirrel can dodge around the tree it strikes him in the head, and, as he falls to the ground, my Ohitika is upon him."

He knelt upon one knee as he talked, his black eyes shining like evening stars.

"Sit down here," said Uncheedah to the boy; "I have something to say to you. You see that you are now almost a man. Observe the game you have brought me! It will not be long before you will leave me, for a warrior must seek opportunities to make him great among his people.

"You must endeavor to equal your father and grandfather," she went on. "They were warriors and feast-makers. But it is not the poor hunter who makes many feasts. Do you not remember the 'Legend of the Feast-Maker,' who gave forty feasts in twelve moons? And have you forgotten the story of the warrior who sought the will of the Great Mystery? Today you will make your first offering to him."

The concluding sentence fairly dilated the eyes of the young hunter, for he felt that a great event was about to occur, in which he would be the principal actor. But Uncheedah resumed her speech.

"You must give up one of your belongings—whichever is dearest to you—for this is to be a sacrificial offering."

This somewhat confused the boy; not that he was selfish, but rather uncertain as to what would be the most appropriate thing to give. Then, too, he supposed that his grandmother referred to his ornaments and playthings only. So he volunteered:

"I can give up my best bow and arrows, and all the paints I have, and—and my bear's claws necklace, grandmother!"

"Are these the things dearest to you?" she demanded.

"Not the bow and arrows, but the paints will be very hard to get, for there are no white people near; and the necklace—it is not easy to get one like it again. I will also give up my otterskin head-dress, if you think that is not enough."

"But think, my boy, you have not yet mentioned the thing that will be a pleasant offering to the Great Mystery."

The boy looked into the woman's face with a puzzled expression.

"I have nothing else as good as those things I have named, grandmother, unless it is my spotted pony; and I am sure that the Great Mystery will not require a little boy to make him so large a gift. Besides, my uncle gave three otter-skins and five eagle-feathers for him and I promised to keep him a long while, if the Blackfeet or the Crows do not steal him."

Uncheedah was not fully satisfied with the boy's free offerings. Perhaps it had not occurred to him what she really wanted. But Uncheedah knew where his affection was vested. His faithful dog, his pet and companion—Hakadah was almost inseparable from the loving beast.

She was sure that it would be difficult to obtain his consent to sacrifice the animal, but she ventured upon a final appeal.

"You must remember," she said, "that in this offering you will call upon him who looks at you from every creation. In the wind you hear him whisper to you. He gives his war-whoop in the thunder. He watches you by day with his eye, the sun; at night, he gazes upon your sleeping countenance through the moon. In short, it is the Mystery of Mysteries, who controls all things to whom you will make your first offering. By this act, you will ask him to grant to you what he has granted to few men. I know you wish to be a great warrior and hunter. I am not prepared to see my Hakadah show any cowardice, for the love of possessions is a woman's trait and not a brave's."

During this speech, the boy had been completely aroused to the spirit of manliness, and in his excitement was willing to give up anything he had—even his pony! But he was unmindful of his friend and companion, Ohitika, the dog! So, scarcely had Uncheedah finished speaking, when he almost shouted:

"Grandmother, I will give up any of my possessions for the offering to the Great Mystery! You may select what you think will be most pleasing to him."

There were two silent spectators of this little dialogue. One was Wahchewin; the other was Ohitika. The woman had been invited to stay, although only a neighbor. The dog, by force of habit, had taken up his usual position by the side of his master when they entered the teepee. Without moving a muscle, save those of his eyes, he had been a very close observer of what passed.

Had the dog but moved once to attract the attention of his little friend, he might have been dissuaded from that impetuous exclamation: "Grandmother, I will give up any of my possessions!"

It was hard for Uncheedah to tell the boy that he must part with his dog, but she was equal to the situation.

"Hakadah," she proceeded cautiously, "you are a young brave. I know, though young, your heart is strong and your courage is great. You will be pleased to give up the dearest thing you have for your first offering. You must give up Ohitika. He is brave; and you, too, are brave. He will not fear death; you will bear his loss bravely. Come—here are four bundles of paints and a filled pipe—let us go to the place."

When the last words were uttered, Hakadah did not seem to hear them. He was simply unable to speak. To a civilized eye, he would have appeared at that moment like a little copper statue. His bright black eyes were fast melting in floods of tears, when he caught his grandmother's eye and recollected her oft-repeated adage: "Tears for woman and the war-whoop for man to drown sorrow!"

He swallowed two or three big mouthfuls of heart-ache and the little warrior was master of the situation.

"Grandmother, my Brave will have to die! Let me tie together two of the prettiest tails of the squirrels that he and I killed this morning, to show to the Great Mystery what a hunter he has been. Let me paint him myself."

This request Uncheedah could not refuse and she left the pair alone for a few minutes, while she went to ask Wacoota to execute Ohitika.

Every Indian boy knows that, when a warrior is about to meet death, he must sing a death dirge. Hakadah thought of his Ohitika as a person who would meet his death without a struggle, so he began to sing a dirge for him, at the same time hugging him tight to himself. As if he were a human being, he whispered in his ear:

"Be brave, my Ohitika! I shall remember you the first time I am upon the war-path in the Ojibway country."

At last he heard Uncheedah talking with a man outside the teepee, so he quickly took up his paints. Ohitika was a jet-black dog, with a silver tip on the end of his tail and on his nose, beside one white paw and a white star upon a protuberance between his ears. Hakadah knew that a man who prepares for death usually paints with red and black. Nature had partially provided Ohitika in this respect, so that only red was required and this Hakadah supplied generously.

Then he took off a piece of red cloth and tied it around the dog's neck; to this he fastened two of the squirrels' tails and a wing from the oriole they had killed that morning.

Just then it occurred to him that good warriors always mourn for their departed friends and the usual mourning was black paint. He loosened his black braided locks, ground a dead coal, mixed it with bear's oil and rubbed it on his entire face.

During this time every hole in the tent was occupied with an eye. Among the lookers-on was his grandmother. She was very near relenting. Had she not feared the wrath of the Great Mystery, she would have been happy to call out to the boy: "Keep your dear dog, my child!"

As it was, Hakadah came out of the teepee with his face looking like an eclipsed moon, leading his beautiful dog, who was even handsomer than ever with the red touches on his specks of white.

It was now Uncheedah's turn to struggle with the storm and burden in her soul. But the boy was emboldened by the people's admiration of his bravery, and did not shed a tear. As soon as she was able to speak, the loving grandmother said:

"No, my young brave, not so! You must not mourn for your first offering. Wash your face and then we will go."

The boy obeyed, submitted Ohitika to Wacoota with a smile, and walked off with his grandmother and Wahchewin.

They followed a well-beaten foot-path leading along the bank of the Assiniboine river, through a beautiful grove of oak, and finally around and under a very high cliff. The murmuring of the river came up from just below. On the opposite side was a perpendicular white cliff, from which extended back a gradual slope of land, clothed with the majestic mountain oak. The scene was impressive and wild.

Wahchewin had paused without a word when the little party reached the edge of the cliff. It had been arranged between her and Uncheedah that she should wait there for Wacoota, who was to bring as far as that the portion of the offering with which he had been entrusted.

The boy and his grandmother descended the bank, following a tortuous foot-path until they reached the water's edge. Then they proceeded to the mouth of an immense cave, some fifty feet above the river, under the cliff. A little stream of limpid water trickled down from a spring within the cave. The little watercourse served as a sort of natural staircase for the visitors. A cool, pleasant atmosphere exhaled from the mouth of the cavern. Really it was a shrine of nature and it is not strange that it was so regarded by the tribe.

A feeling of awe and reverence came to the boy. "It is the home of the Great Mystery," he thought to himself; and the impressiveness of his surroundings made him forget his sorrow.

Very soon Wahchewin came with some difficulty to the steps. She placed the body of Ohitika upon the ground in a life-like position and again left the two alone.

As soon as she disappeared from view, Uncheedah, with all solemnity and reverence, unfastened the leather strings that held the four small bundles of paints and one of tobacco, while the filled pipe was laid beside the dead Ohitika.

She scattered paints and tobacco all about. Again they stood a few moments silently; then she drew a deep breath and began her prayer to the Great Mystery:

"O, Great Mystery, we hear thy voice in the rushing waters below us! We hear thy whisper in the great oaks above! Our spirits are refreshed with thy breath from within this cave. O, hear our prayer! Behold this little boy and bless him! Make him a warrior and a hunter as great as thou didst make his father and grandfather."

And with this prayer the little warrior had completed his first offering.

V

Family Traditions

I. A Visit to Smoky Day

Smoky Day was widely known among us as a preserver of history and legend. He was a living book of the traditions and history of his people. Among his effects were bundles of small sticks, notched and painted. One bundle contained the number of his own years. Another was composed of sticks representing the important events of history, each of which was marked with the number of years since that particular event occurred. For instance, there was the year when so many stars fell from the sky, with the number of years since it happened cut into the wood. Another recorded the appearance of a comet; and from these heavenly wonders the great national catastrophes and victories were reckoned.

But I will try to repeat some of his favorite narratives as I heard them from his own lips. I went to him one day with a piece of tobacco and an eagle-feather; not to buy his Mss., but hoping for the privilege of hearing him tell of some of the brave deeds of our people in remote times.

The tall and large old man greeted me with his usual courtesy and thanked me for my present. As I recall the meeting, I well remember his unusual stature, his slow speech and gracious manner.

"Ah, Ohiyesa!" said he, "my young warrior—for such you will be some day! I know this by your seeking to hear of the great deeds of your ancestors. That is a good sign, and I love to repeat these stories to one who is destined to be a brave man. I do not wish to lull you to sleep with sweet words; but I know the conduct of your paternal ancestors. They have been and are still among the bravest of our tribe. To prove this, I will relate what happened in your paternal grandfather's family, twenty years ago.

"Two of his brothers were murdered by a jealous young man of their own band. The deed was committed without just cause; therefore all the braves were agreed to punish the murderer with death. When your grandfather was approached with this suggestion, he replied that he and the remaining brothers could not condescend to spill the blood of such a wretch, but that the others might do whatever they thought just with the young man. These men were foremost among the warriors of the Sioux, and no one questioned their courage; yet when this calamity was brought upon them by a villain, they refused to touch him! This, my boy, is a test of true bravery. Self-possession and self-control at such a moment is proof of a strong heart.

"You have heard of Jingling Thunder the elder, whose brave deeds are well known to the Villagers of the Lakes. He sought honor 'in the gates of the enemy,' as we often say. The Great Mystery was especially kind to him, because he was obedient.

"Many winters ago there was a great battle, in which Jingling Thunder won his first honors. It was forty winters before the falling of many stars, which event occurred twenty winters after the coming of the black-robed white priest; and that was fourteen winters before the annihilation by our people of thirty lodges of the Sac and Fox Indians. I well remember the latter event—it was just fifty winters ago. However, I will count my sticks again."

So saying, Smoky Day produced his bundle of variously colored sticks, about five inches long. He counted and gave them to me to verify his calculation.

"But you," he resumed, "do not care to remember the winters that have passed. You are young, and care only for the event and the deed. It was very many years ago that this thing happened that I am about to tell you, and yet our people speak of it with as much enthusiasm as if it were only yesterday. Our heroes are always kept alive in the minds of the nation.

"Our people lived then on the east bank of the Mississippi, a little south of where Imnejah-skah, or White Cliff (St. Paul, Minnesota), now stands. After they left Mille Lacs they founded several villages, but finally settled in this spot, whence the tribes have gradually dispersed. Here a battle occurred which surpassed all others in history. It lasted one whole day—the Sacs and Foxes and the Dakotas against the Ojibways.

"An invitation in the usual form of a filled pipe was brought to the Sioux by a brave of the Sac and Fox tribe, to make a general attack upon their common enemy. The Dakota braves quickly signified their willingness in the same manner, and it having been agreed to meet upon the St. Croix river, preparations were immediately begun to despatch a large war-party.

"Among our people there were many tried warriors whose names were known, and every youth of a suitable age was desirous of emulating them. As these young novices issued from every camp and almost every teepee, their mothers, sisters, grandfathers and grandmothers were singing for them the 'strong-heart' songs. An old woman, living with her only grandchild, the remnant of a once large band who had all been killed at three different times by different parties of the Ojibways, was conspicuous among the singers.

"Everyone who heard, cast toward her a sympathetic glance, for it was well known that she and her grandson constituted the remnant of a band of Sioux, and that her song indicated that her precious child had attained the age of a warrior, and was now about to join the war-party, and to seek a just revenge for the annihilation of his family. This was Jingling Thunder, also familiarly known as 'The Little Last.' He was seen to carry with him some family relics in the shape of war-clubs and lances.

"The aged woman's song was something like this:

> *"Go, my brave Jingling Thunder!*
> *Upon the silvery path*
> *Behold that glittering track—*
>
> *"And yet, my child, remember*
> *How pitiful to live*
> *Survivor of the young!*
> *'Stablish our name and kin!"*

"The Sacs and Foxes were very daring and confident upon this occasion. They proposed to the Sioux that they should engage alone with the enemy at first, and let us see how their braves can fight! To this our people assented, and they assembled upon the hills to watch the struggle between their allies and the Ojibways. It seemed to be an equal fight, and for a time no one could tell how the contest would end. Young Jingling Thunder was an impatient spectator, and it was The Milky Way—believed by the Dakotas to be the road travelled by the spirits of departed braves hard to keep him from rushing forward to meet his foes.

"At last a great shout went up, and the Sacs and Foxes were seen to be retreating with heavy loss. Then the Sioux took the field, and were fast winning the day, when fresh reinforcements came from the north for the Ojibways. Up to this time Jingling Thunder had been among the foremost in the battle, and had engaged in several close encounters. But this fresh attack of the Ojibways was unexpected, and the Sioux were somewhat tired. Besides, they had told the Sacs and Foxes to sit upon the hills and rest their weary limbs and take lessons from their friends the Sioux; therefore no aid was looked for from any quarter.

"A great Ojibway chief made a fierce onslaught on the Dakotas. This man Jingling Thunder now rushed forward to meet. The Ojibway boastfully shouted to his warriors that he had met a tender fawn and would reserve to himself the honor of destroying it. Jingling Thunder, on his side, exclaimed that he had met the aged bear of whom he had heard so much, but that he would need no assistance to overcome him.

"The powerful man flashed his tomahawk in the air over the youthful warrior's head, but the brave sprang aside as quick as lightning, and in the same instant speared his enemy to the heart. As the Ojibway chief gave a gasping yell and fell in death, his people lost courage; while the success of the brave Jingling Thunder strengthened the hearts of the Sioux, for they immediately followed up their advantage and drove the enemy out of their territory.

"This was the beginning of Jingling Thunder's career as a warrior. He afterwards performed even greater acts of valor. He became the ancestor of a famous band of the Sioux, of whom your own father, Ohiyesa, was a member. You have doubtless heard his name in connection with many great events. Yet he was a patient man, and was never known to quarrel with one of his own nation."

That night I lay awake a long time committing to memory the tradition I had heard, and the next day I boasted to my playmate, Little Rainbow, about my first lesson from the old storyteller. To this he replied:

"I would rather have Weyuhah for my teacher. I think he remembers more than any of the others. When Weyuhah tells about a battle you can see it yourself; you can even hear the war-whoop," he went on with much enthusiasm.

"That is what his friends say of him; but those who are not his friends say that he brings many warriors into the battle who were not there," I answered indignantly, for I could not admit that old Smoky Day could have a rival.

Before I went to him again Uncheedah had thoughtfully prepared a nice venison roast for the teacher, and I was proud to take him something good to eat before beginning his story.

"How," was his greeting, "so you have begun already, Ohiyesa? Your family were ever feastmakers as well as warriors."

Having done justice to the tender meat, he wiped his knife by sticking it into the ground several times, and put it away in its sheath, after which he cheerfully recommenced:

"It came to pass not many winters ago that Wakinyan-tonka, the great medicine man, had a vision; whereupon a war-party set out for the Ojibway country. There were three brothers of your family among them, all of whom were noted for valor and the chase.

"Seven battles were fought in succession before they turned to come back. They had secured a number of the enemy's birch canoes, and the whole party came floating down the Mississippi, joyous and happy because of their success.

"But one night the war-chief announced that there was misfortune at hand. The next day no one was willing to lead the fleet. The youngest of the three brothers finally declared that he did not fear death, for it comes when least expected and he volunteered to take the lead.

"It happened that this young man had left a pretty maiden behind him, whose choice needlework adorned his quiver. He was very handsome as well as brave.

"At daybreak the canoes were again launched upon the bosom of the great river. All was quiet—a few birds beginning to sing. Just as the sun peeped through the eastern tree-tops a great warcry came forth from the near shores, and there was a rain of arrows. The birchen canoes were pierced, and in the excitement many were capsized.

"The Sioux were at a disadvantage. There was no shelter. Their bowstrings and the feathers on their arrows were wet. The bold Ojibways saw their advantage and pressed closer and closer; but our men fought desperately, half in and half out of the water, until the enemy was forced at last to retreat. Nevertheless that was a sad day for the Wahpeton Sioux; but saddest of all was Winona's fate!

"Morning Star, her lover, who led the canoe fleet that morning, was among the slain. For two days the Sioux braves searched in the water for their dead, but his body was not recovered.

"At home, meanwhile, the people had been alarmed by ill omens. Winona, eldest daughter of the great chief, one day entered her birch canoe alone and paddled up the Mississippi, gazing now into the water around her, now into the blue sky above. She thought she heard some young men giving courtship calls in the distance, just as they do at night when approaching the teepee of the beloved; and she knew the voice of Morning Star well! Surely she could distinguish his call among the others! Therefore she listened yet more intently, and looked skyward as her light canoe glided gently up stream.

"Ah, poor Winona! She saw only six sandhill cranes, looking no larger than mosquitoes, as they flew in circles high up in the sky, going east where all spirits go. Something said to her: 'Those are the spirits of some of the Sioux braves, and Morning Star is among them!' Her eye followed the birds as they traveled in a chain of circles.

"Suddenly she glanced downward. 'What is this?' she screamed in despair. It was Morning Star's body, floating down the river; his quiver, worked by her own hands and now dyed with his blood, lay upon the surface of the water.

"'Ah, Great Mystery! why do you punish a poor girl so? Let me go with the spirit of Morning Star!'

"It was evening. The pale moon arose in the east and the stars were bright. At this very hour the news of the disaster was brought home by a returning scout, and the village was plunged in grief, but Winona's spirit had flown away. No one ever saw her again.

"This is enough for today, my boy. You may come again tomorrow."

II. The Stone Boy

"Ho, mita koda!" (welcome, friend!) was Smoky Day's greeting, as I entered his lodge on the third day. "I hope you did not dream of a watery combat with the Ojibways, after the history I repeated to you yesterday," the old sage continued, with a complaisant smile playing upon his face.

"No," I said, meekly, "but, on the other hand, I have wished that the sun might travel a little faster, so that I could come for another story."

"Well, this time I will tell you one of the kind we call myths or fairy stories. They are about men and women who do wonderful things— things that ordinary people cannot do at all. Sometimes they are not exactly human beings, for they partake of the nature of men and beasts, or of men and gods. I tell you this beforehand, so that you may not ask any questions, or be puzzled by the inconsistency of the actors in these old stories.

"Once there were ten brothers who lived with their only sister, a young maiden of sixteen summers. She was very skilful at her embroidery, and her brothers all had beautifully worked quivers and bows embossed with porcupine quills. They loved and were kind to her, and the maiden in her turn loved her brothers dearly, and was content with her position as their housekeeper. They were great hunters, and scarcely ever remained at home during the day, but when they returned at evening they would relate to her all their adventures.

"One night they came home one by one with their game, as usual, all but the eldest, who did not return. It was supposed by the other brothers that he had pursued a deer too far from the lodge, or perhaps shot more game than he could well carry; but the sister had a presentiment that something dreadful had befallen him. She was partially consoled by the second brother, who offered to find the lost one in the morning.

"Accordingly, he went in search of him, while the rest set out on the hunt as usual. Toward evening all had returned safely, save the brother who went in search of the absent. Again, the next older brother went to look for the others, and he too returned no more. All the young men disappeared one by one in this manner, leaving their sister alone.

"The maiden's sorrow was very great. She wandered everywhere, weeping and looking for her brothers, but found no trace of them. One day she was walking beside a beautiful little stream, whose clear waters went laughing and singing on their way. She could see the gleaming pebbles at the bottom, and one in particular seemed so lovely to her tear-bedimmed eyes, that she stooped and picked it up, dropping it within her skin garment into her bosom. For the first time since her misfortunes she had forgotten herself and her sorrow.

"At last she went home, much happier than she had been, though she could not have told the reason why. On the following day she sought again the place where she had found the pebble, and this time she fell asleep on the banks of the stream, When she awoke, there lay a beautiful babe in her bosom.

"She took it up and kissed it many times. And the child was a boy, but it was heavy like a stone, so she called him a 'Little Stone Boy.' The maiden cried no more, for she was very happy with her baby. The child was unusually knowing, and walked almost from its birth.

"One day Stone Boy discovered the bow and arrows of one of his uncles, and desired to have them; but his mother cried, and said:

"'Wait, my son, until you are a young man.' She made him some little ones, and with these he soon learned to hunt, and killed small game enough to support them both. When he had grown to be a big boy, he insisted upon knowing whose were the ten bows that still hung upon the walls of his mother's lodge.

"At last she was obliged to tell him the sad story of her loss.

"'Mother, I shall go in search of my uncles,' exclaimed the Stone Boy.

"'But you will be lost like them,' she replied, 'and then I shall die of grief.'

"'No, I shall not be lost. I shall bring your ten brothers back to you. Look, I will give you a sign. I will take a pillow, and place it upon end. Watch this, for as long as I am living the pillow will stay as I put it. Mother, give me some food and some moccasins with which to travel!'

"Taking the bow of one of his uncles, with its quiver full of arrows, the Stone Boy departed. As he journeyed through the forest he spoke to every animal he met, asking for news of his lost uncles. Sometimes he called to them at the top of his voice. Once he thought he heard an answer, so he walked in the direction of the sound. But it was only a great grizzly bear who had wantonly mimicked the boy's call. Then Stone Boy was greatly provoked.

"'Was it you who answered my call, you longface?' he exclaimed.

"Upon this the latter growled and said:

"'You had better be careful how you address me, or you may be sorry for what you say!'

"'Who cares for you, you red-eyes, you ugly thing!' the boy replied; whereupon the grizzly immediately set upon him.

"But the boy's flesh became as hard as stone, and the bear's great teeth and claws made no impression upon it. Then he was so dreadfully heavy; and he kept laughing all the time as if he were being tickled, which greatly aggravated the bear. Finally Stone Boy pushed him aside and sent an arrow to his heart.

"He walked on for some distance until he came to a huge fallen pine tree, which had evidently been killed by lightning. The ground near by bore marks of a struggle, and Stone Boy picked up several arrows exactly like those of his uncles, which he himself carried.

"While he was examining these things, he heard a sound like that of a whirlwind, far up in the heavens. He looked up and saw a black speck which grew rapidly larger until it became a dense cloud. Out of it came a flash and then a thunderbolt. The boy was obliged to wink; and when he opened his eyes, behold! a stately man stood before him and challenged him to single combat.

"Stone Boy accepted the challenge and they grappled with one another. The man from the clouds was gigantic in stature and very powerful. But Stone Boy was both strong and unnaturally heavy and hard to hold. The great warrior from the sky sweated from his exertions, and there came a heavy shower. Again and again the lightnings flashed about them as the two struggled there. At last Stone Boy threw his opponent, who lay motionless. There was a murmuring sound throughout the heavens and the clouds rolled swiftly away.

"'Now,' thought the hero, 'this man must have slain all my uncles. I shall go to his home and find out what has become of them.' With this he unfastened from the dead man's scalp-lock a beautiful bit of scarlet down. He breathed gently upon it, and as it floated upward he followed into the blue heavens.

"Away went Stone Boy to the country of the Thunder Birds. It was a beautiful land, with lakes, rivers, plains and mountains. The young adventurer found himself looking down from the top of a high mountain, and the country appeared to be very populous, for he saw lodges all about him as far as the eye could reach. He particularly noticed a majestic tree which towered above all the others, and in its bushy top bore an enormous nest. Stone Boy descended from the mountain and soon arrived at the foot of the tree; but there were no limbs except those at the top and it was so tall that he did not attempt to climb it. He simply took out his bit of down, breathed upon it and floated gently upward.

"When he was able to look into the nest he saw there innumerable eggs of various sizes, and all of a remarkable red color. He was nothing but a boy after all, and had all a boy's curiosity and recklessness. As he was handling the eggs carelessly, his notice was attracted to a sudden confusion in the little village below. All of the people seemed to be running toward the tree. He mischievously threw an egg at them, and in the instant that it broke he saw one of the men drop dead. Then all began to cry out pitifully, 'Give me my heart!'

"'Ah,' exclaimed Stone Boy, exulting, 'so these are the hearts of the people who destroyed my uncles! I shall break them all!'

"And he really did break all of the eggs but four small ones which he took in his hand. Then he descended the tree, and wandered among the silent and deserted lodges in search of some trace of his lost uncles. He found four little boys, the sole survivors of their race, and these he commanded to tell him where their bones were laid.

"They showed him the spot where a heap of bones was bleaching on the ground. Then he bade one of the boys bring wood, a second water, a third stones, and the fourth he sent to cut willow wands for the sweat lodge. They obeyed, and Stone Boy built the lodge, made a fire, heated the stones and collected within the lodge all the bones of his ten uncles.

"As he poured the water upon the hot stones faint sounds could be heard from within the magic bath. These changed to the murmuring of voices, and finally to the singing of medicine songs. Stone Boy opened the door and his ten uncles came forth in the flesh, thanking him and blessing him for restoring them to life. Only the little finger of the youngest uncle was missing. Stone Boy now heartlessly broke the four remaining eggs, and took the little finger of the largest boy to supply the missing bone.

"They all returned to earth again and Stone Boy conducted his uncles to his mother's lodge. She had never slept during his entire absence, but watched incessantly the pillow upon which her boy was wont to rest his head, and by which she was to know of his safety. Going a little in advance of the others, he suddenly rushed forward into her teepee, exclaiming: 'Mother, your ten brothers are coming—prepare a feast!'

"For some time after this they all lived happily together. Stone Boy occupied himself with solitary hunting. He was particularly fond of hunting the fiercer wild animals. He killed them wantonly and brought home only the ears, teeth and claws as his spoil, and with these he played as he laughingly recounted his exploits. His mother and uncles protested, and begged him at least to spare the lives of those animals held sacred by the Dakotas, but Stone Boy relied upon his supernatural powers to protect him from harm.

"One evening, however, he was noticeably silent and upon being pressed to give the reason, replied as follows:

"'For some days past I have heard the animals talking of a conspiracy against us. I was going west the other morning when I heard a crier announcing a general war upon Stone Boy and his people. The crier was a Buffalo, going at full speed from west to east. Again, I heard the Beaver conversing with the Musk-rat, and both said that their services were already promised to overflow the lakes and rivers and cause a destructive flood. I heard, also, the little Swallow holding a secret council with all the birds of the air. He said that he had been appointed a messenger to the Thunder Birds, and that at a certain signal the doors of the sky would be opened and rains descend to drown Stone Boy. Old Badger and the Grizzly Bear are appointed to burrow underneath our fortifications.

"'However, I am not at all afraid for myself, but I am anxious for you, Mother, and for my uncles.'

"'Ugh!' grunted all the uncles, 'we told you that you would get into trouble by killing so many of our sacred animals for your own amusement.

"'But,' continued Stone Boy, 'I shall make a good resistance, and I expect you all to help me.'

"Accordingly they all worked under his direction in preparing for the defence. First of all, he threw a pebble into the air, and behold a great rocky wall around their teepee. A second, third, fourth and fifth pebble became other walls without the first. From the sixth and seventh were formed two stone lodges, one upon the other. The uncles meantime, made numbers of bows and quivers full of arrows, which were ranged at convenient distances along the tops of the walls. His mother prepared great quantities of food and made many moccasins for her boy, who declared that he would defend the fortress alone.

"At last they saw the army of beasts advancing, each tribe by itself and commanded by a leader of extraordinary size. The onset was terrific. They flung themselves against the high walls with savage cries, while the badgers and other burrowing animals ceaselessly worked to undermine them. Stone Boy aimed his sharp arrows with such deadly effect that his enemies fell by thousands. So great was their loss that the dead bodies of the animals formed a barrier higher than the first, and the armies retired in confusion.

"But reinforcements were at hand. The rain fell in torrents; the beavers had dammed all the rivers and there was a great flood. The besieged all retreated into the innermost lodge, but the water poured in through the burrows made by the badgers and gophers, and rose until Stone Boy's mother and his ten uncles were all drowned. Stone Boy himself could not be entirely destroyed, but he was overcome by his enemies and left half buried in the earth, condemned never to walk again, and there we find him to this day.

"This was because he abused his strength, and destroyed for mere amusement the lives of the creatures given him for use only."

VI

Evening in the Lodge

I. Evening in the Lodge

I HAD BEEN SKATING ON that part of the lake where there was an overflow, and came home somewhat cold. I cannot say just how cold it was, but it must have been intensely so, for the trees were cracking all about me like pistol shots. I did not mind, because I was wrapped up in my buffalo robe with the hair inside, and a wide leather belt held it about my loins. My skates were nothing more than strips of basswood bark bound upon my feet.

I had taken off my frozen moccasins and put on dry ones in their places.

"Where have you been and what have you been doing?" Uncheedah asked as she placed before me some roast venison in a wooden bowl. "Did you see any tracks of moose or bear?"

"No, grandmother, I have only been playing at the lower end of the lake. I have something to ask you," I said, eating my dinner and supper together with all the relish of a hungry boy who has been skating in the cold for half a day.

"I found this feather, grandmother, and I could not make out what tribe wear feathers in that shape."

"Ugh, I am not a man; you had better ask your uncle. Besides, you should know it yourself by this time. You are now old enough to think about eagle feathers."

I felt mortified by this reminder of my ignorance. It seemed a reflection on me that I was not ambitious enough to have found all such matters out before.

"Uncle, you will tell me, won't you?" I said, in an appealing tone.

"I am surprised, my boy, that you should fail to recognize this feather. It is a Cree medicine feather, and not a warrior's."

"Then," I said, with much embarrassment, "you had better tell me again, uncle, the language of the feathers. I have really forgotten it all."

The day was now gone; the moon had risen; but the cold had not lessened, for the trunks of the trees were still snapping all around our teepee, which was lighted and warmed by the immense logs which Uncheedah's industry had provided. My uncle, White Foot-print, now undertook to explain to me the significance of the eagle's feather.

"The eagle is the most war-like bird," he began, "and the most kingly of all birds; besides, his feathers are unlike any others, and these are the reasons why they are used by our people to signify deeds of bravery.

"It is not true that when a man wears a feather bonnet, each one of the feathers represents the killing of a foe or even a coup. When a man wears an eagle feather upright upon his head, he is supposed to have counted one of four coups upon his enemy."

"Well, then, a coup does not mean the killing of an enemy?"

"No, it is the after-stroke or touching of the body after he falls. It is so ordered, because oftentimes the touching of an enemy is much more difficult to accomplish than the shooting of one from a distance. It requires a strong heart to face the whole body of the enemy, in order to count the coup on the fallen one, who lies under cover of his kinsmen's fire. Many a brave man has been lost in the attempt.

"When a warrior approaches his foe, dead or alive, he calls upon the other warriors to witness by saying: 'I, Fearless Bear, your brave, again perform the brave deed of counting the first (or second or third or fourth) coup upon the body of the bravest of your enemies.' Naturally, those who are present will see the act and be able to testify to it. When they return, the heralds, as you know, announce publicly all such deeds of valor, which then become a part of the man's war record. Any brave who would wear the eagle's feather must give proof of his right to do so.

"When a brave is wounded in the same battle where he counted his coup, he wears the feather hanging downward. When he is wounded, but makes no count, he trims his feather and in that case, it need not be an eagle feather. All other feathers are merely ornaments. When a warrior wears a feather with a round mark, it means that he slew his enemy. When the mark is cut into the feather and painted red, it means that he took the scalp.

"A brave who has been successful in ten battles is entitled to a war-bonnet; and if he is a recognized leader, he is permitted to wear one with long, trailing plumes. Also those who have counted many coups may tip the ends of the feathers with bits of white or colored down. Sometimes the eagle feather is tipped with a strip of weasel skin; that means the wearer had the honor of killing, scalping and counting the first coup upon the enemy all at the same time.

"This feather you have found was worn by a Cree—it is indiscriminately painted. All other feathers worn by the common Indians mean nothing," he added.

"Tell me, uncle, whether it would be proper for me to wear any feathers at all if I have never gone upon the war-path."

"You could wear any other kind of feathers, but not an eagle's," replied my uncle, "although sometimes one is worn on great occasions by the child of a noted man, to indicate the father's dignity and position."

The fire had gone down somewhat, so I pushed the embers together and wrapped my robe more closely about me. Now and then the ice on the lake would burst with a loud report like thunder. Uncheedah was busy re-stringing one of uncle's old snow-shoes. There were two different kinds that he wore; one with a straight toe and long; the other shorter and with an upturned toe. She had one of the shoes fastened toe down, between sticks driven into the ground, while she put in some new strings and tightened the others. Aunt Four Stars was beading a new pair of moccasins.

Wabeda, the dog, the companion of my boyhood days, was in trouble because he insisted upon bringing his extra bone into the teepee, while Uncheedah was determined that he should not. I sympathized with him, because I saw the matter as he did. If he should bury it in the snow outside, I knew Shunktokecha (the coyote) would surely steal it. I knew just how anxious Wabeda was about his bone. It was a fat bone—I mean a bone of a fat deer; and all Indians know how much better they are than the other kind.

Wabeda always hated to see a good thing go to waste. His eyes spoke words to me, for he and I had been friends for a long time. When I was afraid of anything in the woods, he would get in front of me at once and gently wag his tail. He always made it a point to look directly in my face. His kind, large eyes gave me a thousand assurances. When I was perplexed, he would hang about me until he understood the situation. Many times I believed he saved my life by uttering the dog word in time.

Most animals, even the dangerous grizzly, do not care to be seen when the two-legged kind and his dog are about. When I feared a surprise by a bear or a grey wolf, I would say to Wabeda: "Now, my dog, give your war-whoop:" and immediately he would sit up on his haunches and bark "to beat the band" as you white boys say. When a bear or wolf heard the noise, he would be apt to retreat.

Sometimes I helped Wabeda and gave a warwhoop of my own. This drove the deer away as well, but it relieved my mind.

When he appealed to me on this occasion, therefore, I said: "Come, my dog, let us bury your bone so that no Shunktokecha will take it."

He appeared satisfied with my suggestion, so we went out together.

We dug in the snow and buried our bone wrapped up in a piece of old blanket, partly burned; then we covered it up again with snow. We knew that the coyote would not touch anything burnt. I did not put it up a tree because Wabeda always objected to that, and I made it a point to consult his wishes whenever I could.

I came in and Wabeda followed me with two short rib bones in his mouth. Apparently he did not care to risk those delicacies.

"There," exclaimed Uncheedah, "you still insist upon bringing in some sort of bone!" but I begged her to let him gnaw them inside because it was so cold. Having been granted this privilege, he settled himself at my back and I became absorbed in some specially nice arrows that uncle was making.

"O, uncle, you must put on three feathers to all of them so that they can fly straight," I suggested.

"Yes, but if there are only two feathers, they will fly faster," he answered.

"Woow!" Wabeda uttered his suspicions.

"Woow!" he said again, and rushed for the entrance of the teepee. He kicked me over as he went and scattered the burning embers.

"En na he na!" Uncheedah exclaimed, but he was already outside.

"Wow, wow, wow! Wow, Wow, wow!"

A deep guttural voice answered him.

Out I rushed with my bow and arrows in my hand.

"Come, uncle, come! A big cinnamon bear!" I shouted as I emerged from the teepee.

Uncle sprang out and in a moment he had sent a swift arrow through the bear's heart. The animal fell dead. He had just begun to dig up Wabeda's bone, when the dog's quick ear had heard the sound.

"Ah, uncle, Wabeda and I ought to have at least a little eaglet's feather for this. I too sent my small arrow into the bear before he fell," I exclaimed. "But I thought all bears ought to be in their lodges in the winter time. What was this one doing at this time of the year and night?"

"Well," said my uncle, "I will tell you. Among the tribes, some are naturally lazy. The cinnamon bear is the lazy one of his tribe. He alone

CHARLES A. EASTMAN

sleeps out of doors in the winter and because he has not a warm bed, he is soon hungry. Sometimes he lives in the hollow trunk of a tree, where he has made a bed of dry grass; but when the night is very cold, like tonight, he has to move about to keep himself from freezing and as he prowls around, he gets hungry."

We dragged the huge carcass within our lodge. "O, what nice claws he has, uncle!" I exclaimed eagerly. "Can I have them for my necklace?"

"It is only the old medicine men who wear them regularly. The son of a great warrior who has killed a grizzly may wear them upon a public occasion," he explained.

"And you are just like my father and are considered the best hunter among the Santees and Sissetons. You have killed many grizzlies so that no one can object to my bear's-claws necklace," I said appealingly.

White Foot print smiled. "My boy, you shall have them," he said, "but it is always better to earn them yourself." He cut the claws off carefully for my use.

"Tell me, uncle, whether you could wear these claws all the time?" I asked.

"Yes, I am entitled to wear them, but they are so heavy and uncomfortable," he replied, with a superior air.

At last the bear had been skinned and dressed and we all resumed our usual places. Uncheedah was particularly pleased to have some more fat for her cooking.

"Now, grandmother, tell me the story of the bear's fat. I shall be so happy if you will," I begged.

"It is a good story and it is true. You should know it by heart and gain a lesson from it," she replied. "It was in the forests of Minnesota, in the country that now belongs to the Ojibways. From the Bedawakanton Sioux village a young married couple went into the woods to get fresh venison. The snow was deep; the ice was thick. Far away in the woods they pitched their lonely teepee. The young man was a well-known hunter and his wife a good maiden of the village.

"He hunted entirely on snow-shoes, because the snow was very deep. His wife had to wear snow-shoes too, to get to the spot where they pitched their tent. It was thawing the day they went out, so their path was distinct after the freeze came again.

"The young man killed many deer and bears. His wife was very busy curing the meat and trying out the fat while he was away hunting each day. In the evenings she kept on trying the fat. He sat on one side of the teepee and she on the other.

"One evening, she had just lowered a kettle of fat to cool, and as she looked into the hot fat she saw the face of an Ojibway scout looking down at them through the smoke-hole. She said nothing, nor did she betray herself in any way.

"After a little she said to her husband in a natural voice: 'Marpeetopah, some one is looking at us through the smoke hole, and I think it is an enemy's scout.'

"Then Marpeetopah (Four-skies) took up his bow and arrows and began to straighten and dry them for the next day's hunt, talking and laughing meanwhile. Suddenly he turned and sent an arrow upward, killing the Ojibway, who fell dead at their door.

"'Quick, Wadutah!' he exclaimed; 'you must hurry home upon our trail. I will stay here. When this scout does not return, the warparty may come in a body or send another scout. If only one comes, I can soon dispatch him and then I will follow you. If I do not do that, they will overtake us in our flight.'

"Wadutah (Scarlet) protested and begged to be allowed to stay with her husband, but at last she came away to get reinforcements.

"Then Marpeetopah (Four-skies) put more sticks on the fire so that the teepee might be brightly lit and show him the way. He then took the scalp of the enemy and proceeded on his track, until he came to the upturned root of a great tree. There he spread out his arrows and laid out his tomahawk.

"Soon two more scouts were sent by the Ojibway war-party to see what was the trouble and why the first one failed to come back. He heard them as they approached. They were on snowshoes. When they came close to him, he shot an arrow into the foremost. As for the other, in his effort to turn quickly his snow-shoes stuck in the deep snow and detained him, so Marpeetopah killed them both.

"Quickly he took the scalps and followed Wadutah. He ran hard. But the Ojibways suspected something wrong and came to the lonely teepee, to find all their scouts had been killed. They followed the path of Marpeetopah and Wadutah to the main village, and there a great battle was fought on the ice. Many were killed on both sides. It was after this that the Sioux moved to the Mississippi river."

I was sleepy by this time and I rolled myself up in my buffalo robe and fell asleep.

II. Adventures of My Uncle

IT WAS A BEAUTIFUL FALL day—'a gopher's last look back,' as we used to say of the last warm days of the late autumn. We were encamped beside a wild rice lake, where two months before we had harvested our watery fields of grain, and where we had now returned for the duck-hunting. All was well with us. Ducks were killed in countless numbers, and in the evenings the men hunted deer in canoes by torchlight along the shores of the lake. But alas! life is made up of good times and bad times, and it is when we are perfectly happy that we should expect some overwhelming misfortune.

"So it was that upon this peaceful and still morning, all of a sudden a harsh and terrible war-cry was heard! Your father was then quite a young man, and a very ambitious warrior, so that I was always frightened on his account whenever there was a chance of fighting. But I did not think of your uncle, Mysterious Medicine, for he was not over fifteen at the time; besides, he had never shown any taste for the field.

"Our camp was thrown into great excitement; and as the warriors advanced to meet the enemy, I was almost overcome by the sight of your uncle among them! It was of no use for me to call him back—I think I prayed in that moment to the Great Mystery to bring my boy safely home.

"I shall never forget, as long as I live, the events of that day. Many brave men were killed; among them two of your uncle's intimate friends. But when the battle was over, my boy came back; only his face was blackened in mourning for his friends, and he bore several wounds in his body. I knew that he had proved himself a true warrior.

"This was the beginning of your uncle's career, He has surpassed your father and your grandfather; yes, all his ancestors except Jingling Thunder, in daring and skill."

Such was my grandmother's account of the maiden battle of her third son, Mysterious Medicine. He achieved many other names; among them Big Hunter, Long Rifle and White Footprint. He had a favorite Kentucky rifle which he carried for many years. The stock was several times broken, but he always made another. With this gun he excelled most of his contemporaries in accuracy of aim. He used to call the weapon Ishtahbopopa—a literal translation would be "Pops-the-eye."

My uncle, who was a father to me for ten years of my life, was almost a giant in his proportions, very symmetrical and "straight as an arrow." His face was not at all handsome. He had very quiet and reserved manners and was a man of action rather than of unnecessary words. Behind the veil of Indian reticence he had an inexhaustible fund of wit and humor; but this part of his character only appeared before his family and very intimate friends. Few men know nature more thoroughly than he. Nothing irritated him more than to hear some natural fact misrepresented. I have often thought that with education he might have made a Darwin or an Agassiz.

He was always modest and unconscious of self in relating his adventures. "I have often been forced to realize my danger," he used to say, "but not in such a way as to overwhelm me. Only twice in my life have I been really frightened, and for an instant lost my presence of mind.

"Once I was in full pursuit of a large buck deer that I had wounded. It was winter, and there was a very heavy fall of fresh snow upon the ground. All at once I came upon the body of the deer lying dead on the snow. I began to make a hasty examination, but before I had made any discoveries, I spied the tips of two ears peeping just above the surface of the snow about twenty feet from me. I made a feint of not seeing anything at all, but moved quickly in the direction of my gun, which was leaning against a tree. Feeling, somehow, that I was about to be taken advantage of, I snatched at the same moment my knife from my belt.

"The panther (for such it was) made a sudden and desperate spring. I tried to dodge, but he was too quick for me. He caught me by the shoulder with his great paw, and threw me down. Somehow, he did not retain his hold, but made another leap and again concealed himself in the snow. Evidently he was preparing to make a fresh attack.

"I was partially stunned and greatly confused by the blow; therefore I should have been an easy prey for him at the moment. But when he left me, I came to my senses; and I had been thrown near my gun! I arose and aimed between the tips of his ears—all that was visible of him— and fired. I saw the fresh snow fly from the spot. The panther leaped about six feet straight up into the air, and fell motionless. I gave two good warwhoops, because I had conquered a very formidable enemy. I sat down on the dead body to rest, and my heart beat as if it would knock out all my ribs. I had not been expecting any danger, and that was why I was so taken by surprise.

"The other time was on the plains, in summer. I was accustomed to hunting in the woods, and never before had hunted buffalo on

CHARLES A. EASTMAN

horseback. Being a young man, of course I was eager to do whatever other men did. Therefore I saddled my pony for the hunt. I had a swift pony and a good gun, but on this occasion I preferred a bow and arrows.

"It was the time of year when the buffalo go in large herds and the bulls are vicious. But this did not trouble me at all; indeed, I thought of nothing but the excitement and honor of the chase.

"A vast plain near the Souris river was literally covered with an immense herd. The day was fair, and we came up with them very easily. I had a quiver full of arrows, with a sinew-backed bow.

"My pony carried me in far ahead of all the others. I found myself in the midst of the bulls first, for they are slow. They threw toward me vicious glances, so I hastened my pony on to the cows. Soon I was enveloped in a thick cloud of dust, and completely surrounded by the herd, who were by this time in the act of fleeing, their hoofs making a noise like thunder.

"I could not think of anything but my own situation, which confused me for the moment. It seemed to me to be a desperate one. If my pony, which was going at full speed, should step into a badger hole, I should be thrown to the ground and trampled under foot in an instant. If I were to stop, they would knock me over, pony and all. Again, it seemed as if my horse must fall from sheer exhaustion; and then what would become of me?

"At last I awoke to a calm realization of my own power. I uttered a yell and began to shoot right and left. Very soon there were only a few old bulls who remained near me. The herd had scattered, and I was miles away from my companions.

"It is when we think of our personal danger that we are apt to be at a loss to do the best thing under the circumstances. One should be unconscious of self in order to do his duty. We are very apt to think ourselves brave, when we are most timid. I have discovered that half our young men give the war-whoop when they are frightened, because they fear lest their silence may betray their state of mind. I think we are really bravest when most calm and slow to action."

I urged my uncle to tell me more of his adventures.

"Once," said he, "I had a somewhat peculiar experience, which I think I never related to you before. It was at the time of the fall hunt. One afternoon when I was alone I discovered that I was too far away to reach the camp before dark, so I looked about for a good place to spend the night. This was on the Upper Missouri, before there were any white people there, and when we were in constant danger from wild beasts as well as from hostile Indians. It was necessary to use every precaution and the utmost vigilance.

"I selected a spot which appeared to be well adapted to defense. I had killed two deer, and I hung up pieces of the meat at certain distances in various directions. I knew that any wolf would stop for the meat, A grizzly bear would sometimes stop, but not a mountain lion or a panther. Therefore I made a fire. Such an animal would be apt to attack a solitary fire. There was a full moon that night, which was much in my favor.

"Having cooked and eaten some of the venison, I rolled myself in my blanket and lay down by the fire, taking my Ishtahbopopa for a bed fellow. I hugged it very closely, for I felt that I should need it during the night. I had scarcely settled myself when I heard what seemed to be ten or twelve coyotes set up such a howling that I was quite sure of a visit from them. Immediately after-. ward I heard another sound, which was like the screaming of a small child. This was a porcupine, which had doubtless smelled the meat.

"I watched until a coyote appeared upon a flat rock fifty yards away. He sniffed the air in every direction; then, sitting partly upon his haunches, swung round in a circle with his hind legs sawing the air, and howled and barked in many different keys. It was a great feat! I could not help wondering whether I should be able to imitate him. What had seemed to be the voices of many coyotes was in reality only one animal. His mate soon appeared and then they both seemed satisfied, and showed no signs of a wish to invite another to join them. Presently they both suddenly and quietly disappeared.

"At this moment a slight noise attracted my attention, and I saw that the porcupine had arrived. He had climbed up to the piece of meat nearest me, and was helping himself without any ceremony. I thought it was fortunate that he came, for he would make a good watch dog for me. Very soon, in fact, he interrupted his meal, and caused all his quills to stand out in defiance. I glanced about me and saw the two coyotes slyly approaching my open camp from two different directions.

"I took the part of the porcupine! I rose in a sitting posture, and sent a swift arrow to each of my unwelcome visitors. They both ran away with howls of surprise and pain.

"The porcupine saw the whole from his perch, but his meal was not at all disturbed, for he began eating again with apparent relish. Indeed,

I was soon furnished with another of these unconscious protectors. This one came from the opposite direction to a point where I had hung a splendid ham of venison. He cared to go no further, but seated himself at once on a convenient branch and began his supper.

"The canon above me was full of rocks and trees. From this direction came a startling noise, which caused me more concern than anything I had thus far heard. It sounded much like a huge animal stretching himself, and giving a great yawn which ended in a scream. I knew this for the voice of a mountain lion, and it decided me to perch upon a limb for the rest of the night.

"I got up and climbed into the nearest large tree, taking my weapons with me; but first I rolled a short log of wood in my blanket and laid it in my place by the fire.

"As I got up, the two porcupines began to descend, but I paid no attention to them, and they soon returned to their former positions. Very soon I heard a hissing sound from one of them, and knew that an intruder was near. Two grey wolves appeared.

"I had hung the hams by the ham strings, and they were fully eight feet from the ground. At first the wolves came boldly forward, but the warning of the porcupines caused them to stop, and hesitate to jump for the meat. However, they were hungry, and began to leap savagely for the hams, although evidently they proved good targets for the quills of the prickly ones, for occasionally one of them would squeal and rub his nose desperately against the tree.

"At last one of the wolves buried his teeth too deeply in a tough portion of the flesh, and having jumped to reach it, his own weight made it impossible for him to loosen his upper jaw. There the grey wolf dangled, kicking and yelping, until the tendon of the ham gave way, and both fell heavily to the ground. From my hiding-place I sent two arrows into his body, which ended his life. The other one ran away to a little distance and remained there a long time, as if waiting for her mate.

"I was now very weary, but I had seen many grizzly bears' tracks in the vicinity, and besides, I had not forgotten the dreadful scream of the mountain lion. I determined to continue my watch.

"As I had half expected, there came presently a sudden heavy fall, and at the same time the burning embers were scattered about and the fire almost extinguished. My blanket with the log in it was rolled over several times, amid snarls and growls. Then the assailant of my camp—a panther—leaped back into the thick underbrush, but not before my arrow had penetrated his side. He snarled and tried to bite off the shaft, but after a time became exhausted and lay still.

"I could now distinguish the grey dawn in the east. I was exceedingly drowsy, so I fastened myself by a rope of raw-hide to the trunk of the tree against which I leaned. I was seated on a large limb, and soon fell asleep.

"I was rudely awakened by the report of a gun directly under me. At the same time, I thought some one was trying to shake me off the tree, Instantly I reached for my gun. Alas! it was gone! At the first shake of the tree by my visitor, a grizzly bear, the gun had fallen, and as it was cocked, it went off.

"The bear picked up the weapon and threw it violently away; then he again shook the tree with all his strength. I shouted:

"'I have still a bow and a quiver full of arrows; you had better let me alone.'

"He replied to this with a rough growl. I sent an arrow into his side, and he groaned like a man as he tried hard to pull it out. I had to give him several more before he went a short distance away, and died. It was now daylight, so I came down from my perch. I was stiff, and scarcely able to walk. I found that the bear had killed both of my little friends, the porcupines, and eaten most of the meat.

"Perhaps you wonder, Ohiyesa, why I did not use my gun in the beginning; but I had learned that if I once missed my aim with it, I had no second chance. I have told of this particular adventure, because it was an unusual experience to see so many different animals in one night. I have often been in similar places, and killed one or two. Once a common black bear stole a whole deer from me without waking me. But all this life is fast disappearing, and the world is becoming different."

VII

The End of the Bear Dance

It was one of the superstitions of the Santee Sioux to treat disease from the standpoint of some animal or inanimate thing. That person who, according to their belief, had been commissioned to become a medicine man or a war chief, must not disobey the bear or other creature or thing which gave him his commission. If he ever ventured to do so, the offender must pay for his insubordination with his life, or that of his own child or dearest friend. It was supposed to be necessary that the supernatural orders be carried into effect at a particular age and a certain season of the year. Occasionally a very young man, who excused himself on the ground of youth and modesty, might be forgiven.

One of my intimate friends had been a sufferer from what, I suppose, must have been consumption. He, like myself, had a grandmother in whom he had unlimited faith. But she was a very ambitious and pretentious woman. Among her many claims was that of being a great "medicine woman," and many were deceived by it; but really she was a fraud, for she did not give any medicine, but "conjured" the sick exclusively.

At this time my little friend was fast losing ground, in spite of his grandmother's great pretensions. At last I hinted to him that my grandmother was a herbalist, and a skilful one. But he hinted back to me that 'most any old woman who could dig roots could be a herbalist, and that without a supernatural commission there was no power that could cope with disease. I defended my ideal on the ground that there are supernatural powers in the herbs themselves; hence those who understand them have these powers at their command.

"But," insisted my friend, "one must get his knowledge from the Great Mystery!"

This completely silenced my argument, but did not shake my faith in my grandmother's ability.

Redhorn was a good boy, and I loved him. I visited him often, and found him growing weaker day by day.

"Ohiyesa," he said to me one day, "my grandmother has discovered the cause of my sickness."

I eagerly interrupted him by shouting: "And can she cure you now, Redhorn?"

"Of course," he replied, "she cannot until I have fulfilled the commandment. I have confessed to her that two years ago I received my commission, and I should have made a Bear Dance and proclaimed myself a medicine man last spring, when I had seen thirteen winters. You see, I was ashamed to proclaim myself a medicine man, being so young; and for this I am punished. However, my grandmother says it is not yet too late. But, Ohiyesa, I am as weak now as a rheumatic old man. I can scarcely stand up. They say that I can appoint some one else to act for me. He will be the active bear—I shall have to remain in the hole. Would you, Ohiyesa, be willing to act the bear for me? You know he has to chase the dancers away from his den."

"Redhorn," I replied with much embarrassment, "I should be happy to do anything that I could for you, but I cannot be a bear. I feel that I am not fit. I am not large enough; I am not strong enough; and I don't understand the habits of the animal well enough. I do not think you would be pleased with me as your substitute."

Redhorn finally decided that he would engage a larger boy to perform for him. A few days later, it was announced by the herald that my friend would give a Bear Dance, at which he was to be publicly proclaimed a medicine man. It would be the great event of his short existence, for the disease had already exhausted his strength and vitality. Of course, we all understood that there would be an active youth to exhibit the ferocious nature of the beast after which the dance is named.

The Bear Dance was an entertainment, a religious rite, a method of treating disease—all in one. A strange thing about it was that no woman was allowed to participate in the orgies, unless she was herself the bear.

The den was usually dug about two hundred yards from the camp, on some conspicuous plain. It was about two feet deep and six feet square and over it was constructed an arbor of boughs with four openings. When the bear man sang, all the men and boys would gather and dance about the den; and when he came out and pursued them there was a hasty retreat. It was supposed that whoever touched the bear without being touched by him would overcome a foe in the field. If one was touched, the reverse was to be expected. The thing which caused most anxiety among the dancers was the superstition that if one of them should accidentally trip and fall while pursued by the bear, a sudden death would visit him or his nearest relative.

Boys of my age were disposed to run some risk in this dance; they would take every opportunity to strike at the bear man with a short switch, while the older men shot him with powder. It may as well be admitted that one reason for my declining the honor offered me by my friend Redhorn was that I was afraid of powder, and I much preferred to be one of the dancers and take my chances of touching the bear man without being touched.

It was a beautiful summer's day. The forest behind our camp was sweet with the breath of blossoming flowers. The teepees faced a large lake, which we called Bedatanka. Its gentle waves cooled the atmosphere. The water-fowl disported themselves over its surface, and the birds of passage overhead noisily expressed their surprise at the excitement and confusion in our midst.

The herald, with his brassy voice, again went the rounds, announcing the day's event and the tardy fulfillment of the boy's commission. Then came the bustle of preparation. The out-door toilet of the people was performed with care. I cannot describe just how I was attired or painted, but I am under the impression that there was but little of my brown skin that was not uncovered. The others were similarly dressed in feathers, paint and tinkling ornaments.

I soon heard the tom-tom's doleful sound from the direction of the bear's den, and a few warwhoops from the throats of the youthful warriors. As I joined the motley assembly, I noticed that the bear man's drum was going in earnest, and soon after he began to sing. This was the invitation to the dance.

An old warrior gave the signal and we all started for the den, very much like a group of dogs attacking a stranger. Frantically we yelled and whooped, running around the sheltering arbor in a hop, skip and jump fashion. In spite of the apparent confusion, however, every participant was on the alert for the slightest movement of the bear man.

All of a sudden, a brave gave the warning, and we scattered in an instant over the little plain between the den and our village. Everybody seemed to be running for dear life, and I soon found myself some yards behind the rest. I had gone in boldly, partly because of conversations with certain boys who proposed to participate, and whom I usually outdistanced in foot races. But it seemed that they had not carried out their intentions and I was left alone. I looked back once or twice, although I was pretty busy with my legs, and I imagined that my pursuer, the bear man, looked twice as fearful as a real bear. He was dressed and painted up with a view to terrify the crowd. I did not want the others to guess that I was at all dismayed, so I tried to give the war-whoop; but my throat was so dry at the moment that I am sure I must have given it very poorly.

Just as it seemed that I was about to be overtaken, the dancers who had deserted me suddenly slackened their speed, and entered upon the amusement of tormenting the bear man with gunpowder and switches, with which they touched him far from gently upon his naked body. They now chased him in turn, and he again retreated to his den.

We rested until we heard the tom-tom and the song once more, and then we rushed forth with fresh eagerness to the mimic attack. This time I observed all necessary precautions for my own safety. I started in my flight even before the warning was given, for I saw the bear man gathering himself up to spring upon the dancers. Thus I had plenty of leeway to observe what occurred. The bear man again pursued the yelling and retreating mob, and was dealt with unmercifully by the swift-footed. He became much excited as he desperately chased a middle-aged man, who occasionally turned and fired off his gun, but was suddenly tripped by an ant-hill and fell to the ground, with the other on top of him. The excitement was intense. The bear man returned to his companion, and the dancers gathered in little knots to exchange whispers.

"Is it not a misfortune?" "The most surefooted of us all!" "Will he die?" "Must his beautiful daughter be sacrificed?"

The man who was the subject of all this comment did not speak a word. His head hung down. Finally he raised it and said in a resolute voice:

"We all have our time to go, and when the Great Mystery calls us we must answer as cheerfully as at the call of one of our own war-chiefs here on earth. I am not sad for myself, but my heart is not willing that my Winona (first-born daughter) should be called."

No one replied. Presently the last tom-tom was heard and the dancers rallied once more. The man who had fallen did not join them, but turned to the council lodge, where the wise old men were leisurely enjoying the calumet. They beheld him enter with some surprise; but he threw himself upon a buffalo robe, and resting his head upon his right hand, related what had happened to him. Thereupon the aged men exclaimed as with one voice: "It never fails!" After this, he spoke no more.

Meanwhile, we were hilariously engaged in our last dance, and when the bear man finally retired, we gathered about the arbor to congratulate the sick bear man. But, to our surprise, his companion did not re-enter the den. "He is dead! Redhorn, the bear man, is dead!" We all rushed to the spot. My poor friend, Redhorn, lay dead in the den.

At this instant there was another commotion in the camp. Everybody was running toward the council lodge. A well-known medicine man was loudly summoned thither. But, alas! the man who fell in the dance had suddenly dropped dead.

To the people, another Indian superstition had been verified.

VIII

The Maidens' Feast

There were many peculiar customs among the Indians of an earlier period, some of which tended to strengthen the character of the people and preserve their purity. Perhaps the most unique of these was the annual "feast of maidens." The casual observer would scarcely understand the full force and meaning of this ceremony.

The last one that I ever witnessed was given at Fort Ellis, Manitoba, about the year 1871. Upon the table land just back of the old trading post and fully a thousand feet above the Assiniboine river, surrounded by groves, there was a natural amphitheatre. At one end stood the old fort where since 1830 the northern tribes had come to replenish their powder horns and lead sacks and to dispose of their pelts.

In this spot there was a reunion of all the renegade Sioux on the one hand and of the Assiniboines and Crees, the Canadian tribes, on the other. They were friendly. The matter was not formally arranged, but it was usual for all the tribes to meet here in the month of July.

The Hudson Bay Company always had a good supply of red, blue, green and white blankets, also cloth of brilliant dye, so that when their summer festival occurred the Indians did not lack gayly colored garments. Paints were bought by them at pleasure. Short sleeves were the fashion in their buckskin dresses, and beads and porcupine quills were the principal decorations.

When circumstances are favorable, the Indians are the happiest people in the world. There were entertainments every single day, which everybody had the fullest opportunity to see and enjoy. If anything, the poorest profited the most by these occasions, because a feature in each case was the giving away of savage wealth to the needy in honor of the event. At any public affair, involving the pride and honor of a prominent family, there must always be a distribution of valuable presents.

One bright summer morning, while we were still at our meal of jerked buffalo meat, we heard the herald of the Wahpeton band upon his calico pony as he rode around our circle.

"White Eagle's daughter, the maiden Red Star, invites all the maidens of all the tribes to come and partake of her feast. It will be in the Wahpeton camp, before the sun reaches the middle of the sky. All pure maidens are invited. Red Star also invites the young men to be present, to see that no unworthy maiden should join in the feast."

The herald soon completed the rounds of the different camps, and it was not long before the girls began to gather in great numbers. The fort was fully alive to the interest of these savage entertainments. This particular feast was looked upon as a semi-sacred affair. It would be desecration for any to attend who was not perfectly virtuous. Hence it was regarded as an opportune time for the young men to satisfy themselves as to who were the virtuous maids of the tribe.

There were apt to be surprises before the end of the day. Any young man was permitted to challenge any maiden whom he knew to be unworthy. But woe to him who could not prove his case. It meant little short of death to the man who endeavored to disgrace a woman without cause.

The youths had a similar feast of their own, in which the eligibles were those who had never spoken to a girl in the way of courtship. It was considered ridiculous so to do before attaining some honor as a warrior, and the novices prided themselves greatly upon their self control.

From the various camps the girls came singly or in groups, dressed in bright-colored calicoes or in heavily fringed and beaded buckskin. Their smooth cheeks and the central part of their glossy hair was touched with vermilion. All brought with them wooden basins to eat from. Some who came from a considerable distance were mounted upon ponies; a few, for company or novelty's sake, rode double.

The maidens' circle was formed about a coneshaped rock which stood upon its base. This was painted red. Beside it two new arrows were lightly stuck into the ground. This is a sort of altar, to which each maiden comes before taking her assigned place in the circle, and lightly touches first the stone and then the arrows. By this oath she declares her purity. Whenever a girl approaches the altar there is a stir among the spectators, and sometimes a rude youth would call out:

"Take care! You will overturn the rock, or pull out the arrows!"

Such a remark makes the girls nervous, and especially one who is not sure of her composure.

Immediately behind the maidens' circle is the old women's or chaperons' circle. This second circle is almost as interesting to look at as the inner one. The old women watched every movement of their respective charges with the utmost concern, having previously instructed them how they should conduct themselves in any event.

There was never a more gorgeous assembly of the kind than this one. The day was perfect. The Crees, displaying their characteristic horsemanship, came in groups; the Assiniboines, with their curious pompadour well covered with red paint. The various bands of Sioux all carefully observed the traditional peculiarities of dress and behavior. The attaches of the fort were fully represented at the entertainment, and it was not unusual to see a pale-face maiden take part in the feast.

The whole population of the region had assembled, and the maidens came shyly into the circle. The simple ceremonies observed prior to the serving of the food were in progress, when among a group of Wahpeton Sioux young men there was a stir of excitement. All the maidens glanced nervously toward the scene of the disturbance. Soon a tall youth emerged from the throng of spectators and advanced toward the circle. Every one of the chaperons glared at him as if to deter him from his purpose. But with a steady step he passed them by and approached the maidens' circle.

At last he stopped behind a pretty Assiniboine maiden of good family and said:

"I am sorry, but, according to custom, you should not be here."

The girl arose in confusion, but she soon recovered her self-control.

"What do you mean?" she demanded, indignantly. "Three times you have come to court me, but each time I have refused to listen to you. I turned my back upon you. Twice I was with Mashtinna. She can tell the people that this is true. The third time I had gone for water when you intercepted me and begged me to stop and listen. I refused because I did not know you. My chaperon, Makatopawee, knows that I was gone but a few minutes. I never saw you anywhere else."

The young man was unable to answer this unmistakable statement of facts, and it became apparent that he had sought to revenge himself for her repulse.

"Woo! woo! Carry him out!" was the order of the chief of the Indian police, and the audacious youth was hurried away into the nearest ravine to be chastised.

The young woman who had thus established her good name returned to the circle, and the feast was served. The "maidens' song" was sung, and four times they danced in a ring around the altar. Each maid as she departed once more took her oath to remain pure until she should meet her husband.

CHARLES A. EASTMAN

IX

More Legends

I. A Legend of Devil's Lake

AFTER THE DEATH OF SMOKY Day, old Weyuha was regarded as the greatest story-teller among the Wahpeton Sioux.

"Tell me, good Weyuha, a legend of your father's country," I said to him one evening, for I knew the country which is now known as North Dakota and Southern Manitoba was their ancient hunting-ground. I was prompted by Uncheedah to make this request, after the old man had eaten in our lodge.

"Many years ago," he began, as he passed the pipe to uncle, "we traveled from the Otter-tail to Minnewakan (Devil's Lake). At that time the mound was very distinct where Chotanka lies buried. The people of his immediate band had taken care to preserve it.

"This mound under which lies the great medicine man is upon the summit of Minnewakan Chantay, the highest hill in all that region. It is shaped like an animal's heart placed on its base, with the apex upward.

"The reason why this hill is called Minnewakan Chantay, or the Heart of the Mysterious Land, I will now tell you. It has been handed down from generation to generation, far beyond the memory of our great-grandparents. It was in Chotanka's line of descent that these legends were originally kept, but when he died the stories became everybody's, and then no one believed in them. It was told in this way."

I sat facing him, wholly wrapped in the words of the story-teller, and now I took a deep breath and settled myself so that I might not disturb him by the slightest movement while he was reciting his tale. We were taught this courtesy to our elders, but I was impulsive and sometimes forgot.

"A long time ago," resumed Weyuha, "the red people were many in number, and they inhabited all the land from the coldest place to the region of perpetual summer time. It seemed that they were all of one tongue, and all were friends.

"All the animals were considered people in those days. The buffalo, the elk, the antelope, were tribes of considerable importance. The bears were a smaller band, but they obeyed the mandates of the Great Mystery and were his favorites, and for this reason they have always known more about the secrets of medicine. So they were held in much honor. The wolves, too, were highly regarded at one time. But the buffalo, elk, moose, deer and antelope were the ruling people.

"These soon became conceited and considered themselves very important, and thought no one could withstand them. The buffalo made war upon the smaller tribes, and destroyed many. So one day the Great Mystery thought it best to change the people in form and in language.

"He made a great tent and kept it dark for ten days. Into this tent he invited the different bands, and when they came out they were greatly changed, and some could not talk at all after that. However, there is a sign language given to all the animals that no man knows except some medicine men, and they are under a heavy penalty if they should tell it.

"The buffalo came out of the darkened tent the clumsiest of all the animals. The elk and moose were burdened with their heavy and many-branched horns, while the antelope and deer were made the most defenseless of animals, only that they are fleet of foot. The bear and the wolf were made to prey upon all the others.

"Man was alone then. When the change came, the Great Mystery allowed him to keep his own shape and language. He was king over all the animals, but they did not obey him. From that day, man's spirit may live with the beasts before he is born a man. He will then know the animal language but he cannot tell it in human speech. He always retains his sympathy with them, and can converse with them in dreams.

"I must not forget to tell you that the Great Mystery pitched his tent in this very region. Some legends say that the Minnewakan Chantay was the tent itself, which afterward became earth and stones. Many of the animals were washed and changed in this lake, the Minnewakan, or Mysterious Water. It is the only inland water we know that is salt. No animal has ever swum in this lake and lived."

"Tell me," I eagerly asked, "is it dangerous to man also?"

"Yes," he replied, "we think so; and no Indian has ever ventured in that lake to my knowledge. That is why the lake is called Mysterious," he repeated.

"I shall now tell you of Chotanka. He was the greatest of medicine men. He declared that he was a grizzly bear before he was born in human form." Weyuha seemed to become very earnest when he reached this point in his story. "Listen to Chotanka's life as a grizzly bear."

"'As a bear,' he used to say, 'my home was in sight of the Minnewakan Chantay. I lived with my mother only one winter, and I only saw my father when I was a baby. Then we lived a little way from the Chantay to the north, among scattered oak upon a hillside overlooking the Minnewakan.

"'When I first remember anything, I was playing outside of our home with a buffalo skull that I had found near by. I saw something that looked strange. It walked upon two legs, and it carried a crooked stick, and some red willows with feathers tied to them. It threw one of the willows at me, and I showed my teeth and retreated within our den.

"'Just then my father and mother came home with a buffalo calf. They threw down the dead calf, and ran after the queer thing. He had long hair upon a round head. His face was round, too. He ran and climbed up into a small oak tree.

"'My father and mother shook him down, but not before he had shot some of his red willows into their sides. Mother was very sick, but she dug some roots and ate them and she was well again.' It was thus that Chotanka was first taught the use of certain roots for curing wounds and sickness," Weyuha added.

"'One day'"—he resumed the grizzly's story—"'when I was out hunting with my mother—my father had gone away and never came back—we found a buffalo cow with her calf in a ravine. She advised me to follow her closely, and we crawled along on our knees. All at once mother crouched down under the grass, and I did the same. We saw some of those queer beings that we called "two legs," riding upon big-tail deer (ponies). They yelled as they rode toward us. Mother growled terribly and rushed upon them. She caught one, but many more came with their dogs and drove us into a thicket. They sent the red willows singing after us, and two of them stuck in mother's side. When we got away at last she tried to pull them out, but they hurt her terribly. She pulled them both out at last, but soon after she lay down and died.

"'I stayed in the woods alone for two days then I went around the Minnewakan Chantay on the south side and there made my lonely den. There I found plenty of hazel nuts, acorns and wild plums. Upon the plains the teepsinna were abundant, and I saw nothing of my enemies.

"'One day I found a footprint not unlike my own. I followed it to see who the stranger might be. Upon the bluffs among the oak groves I discovered a beautiful young female gathering acorns. She was of a different band from mine, for she wore a jet black dress.

"'At first she was disposed to resent my intrusion; but when I told her of my lonely life she agreed to share it with me. We came back to my home on the south side of the hill. There we lived happy for a whole year. When the autumn came again Woshepee, for this was her name, said that she must make a warm nest for the winter, and I was left alone again.'

"Now," said Weyuha, "I have come to a part of my story that few people understand. All the long winter Chotanka slept in his den, and with the early spring there came a great thunder storm. He was aroused by a frightful crash that seemed to shake the hills; and lo! a handsome young man stood at his door. He looked, but was not afraid, for he saw that the stranger carried none of those red willows with feathered tips. He was unarmed and smiling.

"'I come,' said he, 'with a challenge to run a race. Whoever wins will be the hero of his kind, and the defeated must do as the winner says thereafter. This is a rare honor that I have brought you. The whole world will see the race. The animal world will shout for you, and the spirits will cheer me on. You are not a coward, and therefore you will not refuse my challenge.'

"'No,' replied Chotanka, after a short hesitation. The young man was fine-looking, but lightly built.

"'We shall start from the Chantay, and that will be our goal. Come, let us go, for the universe is waiting!' impatiently exclaimed the stranger.

"He passed on in advance, and just then an old, old wrinkled man came to Chotanka's door. He leaned forward upon his staff.

"'My son,' he said to him, 'I don't want to make you a coward, but this young man is the greatest gambler of the universe. He has powerful medicine. He gambles for life; be careful! My brothers and I are the only ones who have ever beaten him. But he is safe, for if he is killed he can resurrect himself—I tell you he is great medicine.

"'However, I think that I can save you—listen! He will run behind you all the way until you are within a short distance of the goal. Then he will pass you by in a flash, for his name is ZigZag Fire! (lightning). Here is my medicine.' So speaking, he gave me a rabbit skin and the gum of a certain plant. 'When you come near the goal, rub yourself with the gum, and throw the rabbit skin between you. He cannot pass you.'

"'And who are you, grandfather?' Chotanka inquired.

"'I am the medicine turtle,' the old man replied. 'The gambler is a spirit from heaven, and those whom he outruns must shortly die. You have heard, no doubt, that all animals know beforehand when they are to be killed; and any man who understands these mysteries may also know when he is to die.'

"The race was announced to the world. The buffalo, elk, wolves and all the animals came to look on. All the spirits of the air came also to cheer for their comrade. In the sky the trumpet was sounded—the great medicine drum was struck. It was the signal for a start. The course was around the Minnewakan. (That means around the earth or the ocean.) Everywhere the multitude cheered as the two sped by.

"The young man kept behind Chotanka all the time until they came once more in sight of the Chantay. Then he felt a slight shock and he threw his rabbit skin back. The stranger tripped and fell. Chotanka rubbed himself with the gum, and ran on until he reached the goal. There was a great shout that echoed over the earth, but in the heavens there was muttering and grumbling. The referee declared that the winner would live to a good old age, and Zig-Zag Fire promised to come at his call. He was indeed great medicine," Weyuha concluded.

"But you have not told me how Chotanka became a man," I said.

"One night a beautiful woman came to him in his sleep. She enticed him into her white teepee to see what she had there. Then she shut the door of the teepee and Chotanka could not get out. But the woman was kind and petted him so that he loved to stay in the white teepee. Then it was that he became a human born. This is a long story, but I think, Ohiyesa, that you will remember it," said Weyuha, and so I did.

II. Manitoshaw's Hunting

IT WAS IN THE WINTER, in the Moon of Difficulty (January). We had eaten our venison roast for supper, and the embers were burning brightly. Our teepee was especially cheerful. Uncheedah sat near the entrance, my uncle and his wife upon the opposite side, while I with my pets occupied the remaining space.

Wabeda, the dog, lay near the fire in a half doze, watching out of the corners of his eyes the tame raccoon, which snuggled back against the walls of the teepee, his shrewd brain, doubtless, concocting some mischief for the hours of darkness. I had already recited a legend of our people. All agreed that I had done well. Having been generously praised, I was eager to earn some more compliments by learning a new one, so I begged my uncle to tell me a story. Musingly he replied:

"I can give you a Sioux-Cree tradition," and immediately began:

"Many winters ago, there were six teepees standing on the southern slope of Moose mountain in the Moon of Wild Cherries (September). The men to whom these teepees belonged had been attacked by the Sioux while hunting buffalo, and nearly all killed. Two or three who managed to get home to tell their sad story were mortally wounded, and died soon afterward. There was only one old man and several small boys left to hunt and provide for this unfortunate little band of women and children.

"They lived upon teepsinna (wild turnips) and berries for many days. They were almost famished for meat. The old man was too feeble to hunt successfully. One day in this desolate camp a young Cree maiden—for such they were—declared that she could no longer sit still and see her people suffer. She took down her dead father's second bow and quiver full of arrows, and begged her old grandmother to accompany her to Lake Wanagiska, where she knew that moose had oftentimes been found. I forgot to tell you that her name was Manitoshaw.

"This Manitoshaw and her old grandmother, Nawakewee, took each a pony and went far up into the woods on the side of the mountain. They pitched their wigwam just out of sight of the lake, and hobbled their ponies. Then the old woman said to Manitoshaw:

"'Go, my granddaughter, to the outlet of the Wanagiska, and see if there are any moose tracks there. When I was a young woman, I came here with your father's father, and we pitched our tent near this spot. In the night there came three different moose. Bring me leaves of the birch and cedar twigs; I will make medicine for moose,' she added.

"Manitoshaw obediently disappeared in the woods. It was a grove of birch and willow, with two good springs. Down below was a marshy place. Nawakewee had bidden the maiden look for nibbled birch and willow twigs, for the moose loves to eat them, and to have her arrow ready upon the bow-string. 'I have seen this very place many a time,' added my uncle, and this simple remark gave to the story an air of reality.

"The Cree maiden went first to the spring, and there found fresh tracks of the animal she sought. She gathered some cedar berries and chewed them, and rubbed some of them on her garments so that the moose might not scent her. The sun was already set, and she felt she must return to Nawakewee.

"Just then Hinhankaga, the hooting owl, gave his doleful night call. The girl stopped and listened attentively.

"'I thought it was a lover's call,' she whispered to herself. A singular challenge pealed across the lake. She recognized the alarm call of the loon, and fancied that the bird might have caught a glimpse of her game.

"Soon she was within a few paces of the temporary lodge of pine boughs and ferns which the grandmother had constructed. The old woman met her on the trail.

"'Ah, my child, you have returned none too soon. I feared you had ventured too far away; for the Sioux often come to this place to hunt. You must not expose yourself carelessly on the shore.'

"As the two women lay down to sleep they could hear the ponies munch the rich grass in an open spot near by. Through the smoke hole of the pine-bough wigwam Manitoshaw gazed up into the starry sky, and dreamed of what she would do on the morrow when she should surprise the wily moose. Her grandmother was already sleeping so noisily that it was enough to scare away the game. At last the maiden, too, lost herself in sleep.

"Old Nawakewee awoke early. First of all she made a fire and burned cedar and birch so that the moose might not detect the human smell. Then she quickly prepared a meal of wild turnips and berries, and awoke the maiden, who was surprised to see that the sun was already up. She ran down to the spring and hastily splashed handsful of the cold water in her face; then she looked for a moment in its mirror-like surface. There was the reflection of two moose by the open shore and beyond them Manitoshaw seemed to see a young man standing. In another moment all three had disappeared.

"'What is the matter with my eyes? I am not fully awake yet, and I imagine things. Ugh, it is all in my eyes,' the maiden repeated to herself. She hastened back to Nawakewee. The vision was so unexpected and so startling that she could not believe in its truth, and she said nothing to the old woman.

"Breakfast eaten, Manitoshaw threw off her robe and appeared in her scantily cut gown of buckskin with long fringes, and moccasins and leggings trimmed with quills of the porcupine. Her father's bow and quiver were thrown over one shoulder, and the knife dangled from her belt in its handsome sheath. She ran breathlessly along the shore toward the outlet.

"Way off near the island Medoza the loon swam with his mate, occasionally uttering a cry of joy. Here and there the playful Hogan, the trout, sprang gracefully out of the water, in a shower of falling dew. As the maiden hastened along she scared up Wadawasee, the kingfisher, who screamed loudly.

"'Stop, Wadawasee, stop—you will frighten my game!'

"At last she had reached the outlet. She saw at once that the moose had been there during the night. They had torn up the ground and broken birch and willow twigs in a most disorderly way."

"Ah!" I exclaimed, "I wish I had been with Manitoshaw then!"

"Hush, my boy; never interrupt a storyteller."

I took a stick and began to level off the ashes in front of me, and to draw a map of the lake, the outlet, the moose and Manitoshaw. Away off to one side was the solitary wigwam, Nawakewee and the ponies.

"Manitoshaw's heart was beating so loud that she could not hear anything," resumed my uncle. "She took some leaves of the wintergreen and chewed them to calm herself. She did not forget to throw in passing a pinch of pulverized tobacco and paint into the spring for Manitou, the spirit.

"Among the twinkling leaves of the birch her eye was caught by a moving form, and then another. She stood motionless, grasping her heavy bow. The moose, not suspecting any danger, walked leisurely toward the spring. One was a large female moose; the other a yearling.

"As they passed Manitoshaw, moving so naturally and looking so harmless, she almost forgot to let fly an arrow. The mother moose seemed to look in her direction, but did not see her. They had fairly passed her hiding-place when she stepped forth and sent a swift arrow into the side of the larger moose. Both dashed into the thick woods, but it was too late. The Cree maiden had already loosened her second arrow. Both fell dead before reaching the shore."

"Uncle, she must have had a splendid aim, for in the woods the many little twigs make an arrow bound off to one side," I interrupted in great excitement.

"Yes, but you must remember she was very near the moose."

"It seems to me, then, uncle, that they must have scented her, for you have told me that they possess the keenest nose of any animal," I persisted.

"Doubtless the wind was blowing the other way. But, nephew, you must let me finish my story.

"Overjoyed by her success, the maiden hastened back to Nawakawee, but she was gone! The ponies were gone, too, and the wigwam of branches had been demolished. While Manitoshaw stood there, frightened and undecided what to do, a soft voice came from behind a neighboring thicket:

"'Manitoshaw! Manitoshaw! I am here!'

"She at once recognized, the voice and found it to be Nawakeewee, who told a strange story. That morning a canoe had crossed the Wanagiska carrying two men. They were Sioux. The old grandmother had seen them coming, and to deceive them she at once pulled down her temporary wigwam, and drove the ponies off toward home. Then she hid herself in the bushes near by, for she knew that Manitoshaw must return there.

"'Come, my granddaughter, we must hasten home by another way,' cried the old woman.

"But the maiden said, 'No, let us go first to my two moose that I killed this morning and take some meat with us.'

"'No, no, my child; the Sioux are cruel. They have killed many of our people. If we stay here they will find us. I fear, I fear them, Manitoshaw!'

"At last the brave maid convinced her grandmother, and the more easily as she too was hungry for meat. They went to where the big game lay among the bushes, and began to dress the moose."

"I think, if I were they, I would hide all day. I would wait until the Sioux had gone; then I would go back to my moose," I interrupted for the third time.

"I will finish the story first; then you may tell us what you would do," said my uncle reprovingly.

"The two Sioux were father and son. They too had come to the lake for moose; but as the game usually retreated to the island, Chatansapa had landed his son Kangiska to hunt them on the shore while he returned in his canoe to intercept their flight. The young man sped along the sandy beach and soon discovered their tracks. He followed them up and found blood on the trail. This astonished him. Cautiously he followed on until he found them both lying dead. He examined them and found that in each moose there was a single Cree arrow. Wishing to surprise the hunter if possible, Kangiska lay hidden in the bushes.

"After a little while the two women returned to the spot. They passed him as close as the moose had passed the maiden in the morning. He saw at once that the maiden had arrows in her quiver like those that had slain the big moose. He lay still.

"Kangiska looked upon the beautiful Cree maiden and loved her. Finally he forgot himself and made a slight motion. Manitoshaw's quick eye caught the little stir among the bushes, but she immediately looked the other way and Kangiska believed that she had not seen anything, At last her eyes met his, and something told both that all was well. Then the maiden smiled, and the young man could not remain still any longer. He arose suddenly and the old woman nearly fainted from fright. But Manitoshaw said:

"'Fear not, grandmother; we are two and he is only one.'

"While the two women continued to cut up the meat, Kangiska made a fire by rubbing cedar chips together, and they all ate of the moose meat. Then the old woman finished her work, while the young people sat down upon a log in the shade, and told each other all their minds.

"Kangiska declared by signs that he would go home with Manitoshaw to the Cree camp, for he loved her. They went home, and the young man hunted for the unfortunate Cree band during the rest of his life.

"His father waited a long time on the island and afterward searched the shore, but never saw him again. He supposed that those footprints he saw were made by Crees who had killed his son."

"Is that story true, uncle?" I asked eagerly.

"'Yes, the facts are well known. There are some Sioux mixed bloods among the Crees to this day who are descendants of Kangiska."

X

Indian Life and Adventure

I. Life in the Woods

THE MONTH OF SEPTEMBER RECALLS to every Indian's mind the season of the fall hunt. I remember one such expedition which is typical of many. Our party appeared on the northwestern side of Turtle mountain; for we had been hunting buffaloes all summer, in the region of the Mouse river, between that mountain and the upper Missouri.

As our cone-shaped teepees rose in clusters along the outskirts of the heavy forest that clothes the sloping side of the mountain, the scene below was gratifying to a savage eye. The rolling yellow plains were checkered with herds of buffaloes. Along the banks of the streams that ran down from the mountains were also many elk, which usually appear at morning and evening, and disappear into the forest during the warmer part of the day. Deer, too, were plenty, and the brooks were alive with trout. Here and there the streams were dammed by the industrious beaver.

In the interior of the forest there were lakes with many islands, where moose, elk, deer and bears were abundant. The water-fowl were wont to gather here in great numbers, among them the crane, the swan, the loon, and many of the smaller kinds. The forest also was filled with a great variety of birds. Here the partridge drummed his loudest, while the whippoorwill sang with spirit, and the hooting owl reigned in the night.

To me, as a boy, this wilderness was a paradise. It was a land of plenty. To be sure, we did not have any of the luxuries of civilization, but we had every convenience and opportunity and luxury of Nature. We had also the gift of enjoying our good fortune, whatever dangers might lurk about us; and the truth is that we lived in blessed ignorance of any life that was better than our own.

As soon as hunting in the woods began, the customs regulating it were established. The council teepee no longer existed. A hunting bonfire was kindled every morning at day-break, at which each brave must appear and report. The man who failed to do this before the party set out on the day's hunt was harassed by ridicule. As a rule, the hunters started before sunrise, and the brave who was announced throughout the camp as the first one to return with a deer on his back, was a man to be envied.

The legend-teller, old Smoky Day, was chosen herald of the camp, and it was he who made the announcements. After supper was ended, we heard his powerful voice resound among the teepees in the forest. He would then name a man to kindle the bonfire the next morning. His suit of fringed buckskin set off his splendid physique to advantage.

Scarcely had the men disappeared in the woods each morning than all the boys sallied forth, apparently engrossed in their games and sports, but in reality competing actively with one another in quickness of observation. As the day advanced, they all kept the sharpest possible lookout. Suddenly there would come the shrill "Woo-coohoo!" at the top of a boy's voice, announcing the bringing in of a deer. Immediately all the other boys took up the cry, each one bent on getting ahead of the rest. Now we all saw the brave Wacoota fairly bent over by his burden, a large deer which he carried on his shoulders. His fringed buckskin shirt was besprinkled with blood. He threw down the deer at the door of his wife's mother's home, according to custom, and then walked proudly to his own. At the door of his father's teepee he stood for a moment straight as a pine-tree, and then entered.

When a bear was brought in, a hundred or more of these urchins were wont to make the woods resound with their voices: "Wah! wah! wah! Wah! wah! wah! The brave White Rabbit brings a bear! Wah! wah! wah!"

All day these sing-song cheers were kept up, as the game was brought in. At last, toward the close of the afternoon, all the hunters had returned, and happiness and contentment reigned absolute, in a fashion which I have never observed among the white people, even in the best of circumstances. The men were lounging and smoking; the women actively engaged in the preparation of the evening meal, and the care of the meat. The choicest of the game was cooked and offered to the Great Mystery, with all the accompanying ceremonies. This we called the "medicine feast." Even the women, as they lowered the boiling pot, or the fragrant roast of venison ready to serve, would first whisper: "Great Mystery, do thou partake of this venison, and still be gracious!" This was the commonly said "grace."

Everything went smoothly with us, on this occasion, when we first entered the woods. Nothing was wanting to our old way of living. The killing of deer and elk and moose had to be stopped for a time, since meat was so abundant that we had no use for them any longer. Only the hunting for pelts, such as those of the bear, beaver, marten, and otter was continued. But whenever we lived in blessed abundance, our braves were wont to turn their thoughts to other occupations—especially the hot-blooded youths whose ambition it was to do something noteworthy.

At just such moments as this there are always a number of priests in readiness, whose vocation it is to see into the future, and each of whom consults his particular interpreter of the Great Mystery. (This ceremony is called by the white people "making medicine.") To the priests the youthful braves hint their impatience for the war-path. Soon comes the desired dream or prophecy or vision to favor their departure.

Our young men presently received their sign, and for a few days all was hurry and excitement. On the appointed morning we heard the songs of the warriors and the wailing of the women, by which they bade adieu to each other, and the eligible braves, headed by an experienced man—old Hotanka or Loud-Voiced Raven—set out for the Gros Ventre country.

Our older heads, to be sure, had expressed some disapproval of the undertaking, for the country in which we were roaming was not our own, and we were likely at any time to be taken to task by its rightful owners. The plain truth of the matter was that we were intruders. Hence the more thoughtful among us preferred to be at home, and to achieve what renown they could get by defending their homes and families. The young men, however, were so eager for action and excitement that they must needs go off in search of it.

From the early morning when these braves left us, led by the old war-priest, Loud-Voiced Raven, the anxious mothers, sisters and sweethearts counted the days. Old Smoky Day would occasionally get up early in the morning, and sing a "strong-heart" song for his absent grandson. I still seem to hear the hoarse, cracked voice of the ancient singer as it resounded among the woods. For a long time our roving community enjoyed unbroken peace, and we were spared any trouble or disturbance. Our hunters often brought in a deer or elk or bear for fresh meat. The beautiful lakes furnished us with fish and wild-fowl for variety. Their placid waters, as the autumn advanced, reflected the variegated colors of the changing foliage.

It is my recollection that we were at this time encamped in the vicinity of the "Turtle Mountain's Heart." It is to the highest cone-shaped peak that the Indians aptly give this appellation. Our camping-ground for two months was within a short distance of the peak, and the men made it a point to often send one of their number to the top. It was understood between them and the war party that we were to remain near this spot; and on their return trip the latter were to give the "smoke sign," which we would answer from the top of the hill.

One day, as we were camping on the shore of a large lake with several islands, signs of moose were discovered, and the men went off to them on rafts, carrying their flint-lock guns in anticipation of finding two or three of the animals. We little fellows, as usual, were playing down by the sandy shore, when we spied what seemed like the root of a great tree floating toward us. But on a closer scrutiny we discovered our error. It was the head of a huge moose, swimming for his life! Fortunately for him, none of the men had remained at home.

According to our habit, we little urchins disappeared in an instant, like young prairie chickens, in the long grass. I was not more than eight years old, yet I tested the strength of my bowstring and adjusted my sharpest and best arrow for immediate service. My heart leaped violently as the homely but imposing animal neared the shore. I was undecided for a moment whether I would not leave my hiding-place and give a war-whoop as soon as he touched the sand. Then I thought I would keep still and let him have my boy weapon; and the only regret that I had was that he would, in all probability, take it with him, and I should be minus one good arrow.

"Still," I thought, "I shall claim to be the smallest boy whose arrow was ever carried away by a moose." That was enough. I gathered myself into a bunch, all ready to spring. As the long-legged beast pulled himself dripping out of the water, and shook off the drops from his long hair, I sprang to my feet. I felt some of the water in my face! I gave him my sharpest arrow with all the force I could master, right among the floating ribs. Then I uttered my warwhoop.

The moose did not seem to mind the miniature weapon, but he was very much frightened by our shrill yelling. He took to his long legs, and in a minute was out of sight.

The leaves had now begun to fall, and the heavy frosts made the nights very cold. We were forced to realize that the short summer of that region had said adieu! Still we were gay and lighthearted, for we had plenty of provisions, and no misfortune had yet overtaken us in our wanderings over the country for nearly three months.

One day old Smoky Day returned from the daily hunt with an alarm. He had seen a sign—a "smoke sign." This had not appeared in the quarter that they were anxiously watching—it came from the east. After a long consultation among the men, it was concluded from the nature and duration of the smoke that it proceeded from an accidental fire. It was further surmised that the fire was not made by Sioux, since it was out of their country, but by a war-party of Ojibways, who were accustomed to use matches when lighting their pipes, and to throw them carelessly away. It was thought that a little time had been spent in an attempt to put it out.

The council decreed that a strict look-out should be established in behalf of our party. Every day a scout was appointed to reconnoitre in the direction of the smoke. It was agreed that no gun should be fired for twelve days. All our signals were freshly rehearsed among the men. The women and old men went so far as to dig little convenient holes around their lodges, for defense in case of a sudden attack. And yet an Ojibway scout would not have suspected, from the ordinary appearance of the camp, that the Sioux had become aware of their neighborhood! Scouts were stationed just outside of the village at night. They had been so trained as to rival an owl or a cat in their ability to see in the dark.

The twelve days passed by, however, without bringing any evidence of the nearness of the supposed Ojibway war-party, and the "lookout" established for purposes of protection was abandoned. Soon after this, one morning at dawn, we were aroused by the sound of the unwelcome warwhoop. Although only a child, I sprang up and was about to rush out, as I had been taught to do; but my good grandmother pulled me down, and gave me a sign to lay flat on the ground. I sharpened my ears and lay still.

All was quiet in camp, but at some little distance from us there was a lively encounter. I could distinctly hear the old herald, shouting and yelling in exasperation. "Whoo! whoo!" was the signal of distress, and I could almost hear the pulse of my own blood-vessels.

Closer and closer the struggle came, and still the women appeared to grow more and more calm. At last a tremendous charge by the Sioux put the enemy to flight; there was a burst of yelling; alas! my friend and teacher, old Smoky Day, was silent. He had been pierced to the heart by an arrow from the Ojibways.

Although successful, we had lost two of our men, Smoky Day and White Crane, and this incident, although hardly unexpected, darkened our peaceful sky. The camp was filled with songs of victory, mingled with the wailing of the relatives of the slain. The mothers of the youths who were absent on the war-path could no longer conceal their anxiety.

One frosty morning—for it was then near the end of October—the weird song of a solitary brave was heard. In an instant the camp was thrown into indescribable confusion. The meaning of this was clear as day to everybody—all of our war-party were killed, save the one whose mournful song announced the fate of his companions. The lonely warrior was Bald Eagle.

The village was convulsed with grief; for in sorrow, as in joy, every Indian shares with all the others. The old women stood still, wherever they might be, and wailed dismally, at intervals chanting the praises of the departed warriors. The wives went a little way from their teepees and there audibly mourned; but the young maidens wandered further away from the camp, where no one could witness their grief. The old men joined in the crying and singing. To all appearances the most unmoved of all were the warriors, whose tears must be poured forth in the country of the enemy to embitter their vengeance. These sat silently within their lodges, and strove to conceal their feelings behind a stoical countenance; but they would probably have failed had not the soothing weed come to their relief.

The first sad shock over, then came the change of habiliments. In savage usage, the outward expression of mourning surpasses that of civilization. The Indian mourner gives up all his good clothing, and contents himself with scanty and miserable garments. Blankets are cut in two, and the hair is cropped short. Often a devoted mother would scarify her arms or legs; a sister or a young wife would cut off all her beautiful hair and disfigure herself by undergoing hardships. Fathers and brothers blackened their faces, and wore only the shabbiest garments. Such was the spectacle that our people presented when the bright autumn was gone and the cold shadow of winter and misfortune had fallen upon us. "We must suffer," said they—"the Great Mystery is offended."

II. A Winter Camp

WHEN I WAS ABOUT TWELVE years old we wintered upon the Mouse river, west of Turtle mountain. It was one of the coldest winters I ever knew, and was so regarded by the old men of the tribe. The summer before there had been plenty of buffalo upon that side of the Missouri, and our people had made many packs of dried buffalo meat and cached them in different places, so that they could get them in case of need. There were many black-tailed deer and elk along the river, and grizzlies were to be found in the open country. Apparently there was no danger of starvation, so our people thought to winter there; but it proved to be a hard winter.

There was a great snow-fall, and the cold was intense. The snow was too deep for hunting, and the main body of the buffalo had crossed the Missouri, where it was too far to go after them. But there were some smaller herds of the animals scattered about in our vicinity, therefore there was still fresh meat to be had, but it was not secured without a great deal of difficulty.

No ponies could be used. The men hunted on snow-shoes until after the Moon of Sore Eyes (March), when after a heavy thaw a crust was formed on the snow which would scarcely hold a man. It was then that our people hunted buffalo with dogs—an unusual expedient.

Sleds were made of buffalo ribs and hickory saplings, the runners bound with rawhide with the hair side down. These slipped smoothly over the icy crust. Only small men rode on the sleds. When buffalo were reported by the hunting-scouts, everybody had his dog team ready. All went under orders from the police, and approached the herd under cover until they came within charging distance.

The men had their bows and arrows, and a few had guns. The huge animals could not run fast in the deep snow. They all followed a leader, trampling out a narrow path. The dogs with their drivers soon caught up with them on each side, and the hunters brought many of them down.

I remember when the party returned, late in the night. The men came in single file, well loaded, and each dog following his master with an equally heavy load. Both men and animals were white with frost.

We boys had waited impatiently for their arrival. As soon as we spied them coming a buffalo hunting whistle was started, and every urchin in the village added his voice to the weird sound, while the dogs who had been left at home joined with us in the chorus. The men, wearing their buffalo moccasins with the hair inside and robes of the same, came home hungry and exhausted.

It is often supposed that the dog in the Indian camp is a useless member of society, but it is not so in the wild life. We found him one of the most useful of domestic animals, especially in an emergency.

While at this camp a ludicrous incident occurred that is still told about the camp-fires of the Sioux. One day the men were hunting on snow-shoes, and contrived to get within a short distance of the buffalo before they made the attack. It was impossible to run fast, but the huge animals were equally unable to get away. Many were killed. Just as the herd reached an open plain one of the buffaloes stopped and finally lay down. Three of the men who were pursuing him shortly came up. The animal was severely wounded, but not dead.

"I shall crawl up to him from behind and stab him," said Wamedee; "we cannot wait here for him to die." The others agreed. Wamedee was not considered especially brave; but he took out his knife and held it between his teeth. He then approached the buffalo from behind and suddenly jumped astride his back.

The animal was dreadfully frightened and struggled to his feet. Wamedee's knife fell to the ground, but he held on by the long shaggy hair. He had a bad seat, for he was upon the buffalo's hump. There was no chance to jump off; he had to stay on as well as he could.

"Hurry! hurry! shoot! shoot!" he screamed, as the creature plunged and kicked madly in the deep snow. Wamedee's face looked deathly, they said; but his two friends could not help laughing. He was still calling upon them to shoot, but when the others took aim he would cry: "Don't shoot! don't shoot! you will kill me!" At last the animal fell down with him; but Wamedee's two friends also fell down exhausted with laughter. He was ridiculed as a coward thereafter.

It was on this very hunt that the chief Mato was killed by a buffalo. It happened in this way. He had wounded the animal, but not fatally; so he shot two more arrows at him from a distance. Then the buffalo became desperate and charged upon him. In his flight Mato was tripped by sticking one of his snow-shoes into a snowdrift, from which he could not extricate himself in time. The bull gored him to death. The creek upon which this happened is now called Mato creek.

A little way from our camp there was a log village of French Canadian half-breeds, but the two villages did not intermingle. About the Moon of Difficulty (January) we were initiated into some of the peculiar customs of our neighbors. In the middle of the night there was a firing of guns throughout their village. Some of the people thought they had been attacked, and went over to assist them, but to their surprise they were told that this was the celebration of the birth of the new year!

Our men were treated to minnewakan or "spirit water," and they came home crazy and foolish. They talked loud and sang all the rest of the night. Finally our head chief ordered his young men to tie these men up and put them in a lodge by themselves. He gave orders to untie them "when the evil spirit had gone away."

During the next day all our people were invited to attend the half-breeds' dance. I never knew before that a new year begins in mid-winter. We had always counted that the year ends when the winter ends, and a new year begins with the new life in the springtime.

I was now taken for the first time to a white man's dance in a log house. I thought it was the dizziest thing I ever saw. One man sat in a corner, sawing away at a stringed board, and all the while he was stamping the floor with his foot and giving an occasional shout. When he called out, the dancers seemed to move faster.

The men danced with women—something that we Indians never do—and when the man in the corner shouted they would swing the women around. It looked very rude to me, as I stood outside with the other boys and peeped through the chinks in the logs. At one time a young man and woman facing each other danced in the middle of the floor. I thought they would surely wear their moccasins out against the rough boards; but after a few minutes they were relieved by another couple.

Then an old man with long curly hair and a fox-skin cap danced alone in the middle of the room, slapping the floor with his moccasined foot in a lightning fashion that I have never seen equalled. He seemed to be a leader among them. When he had finished, the old man invited our principal chief into the middle of the floor, and after the Indian had given a great whoop, the two drank in company. After this, there was so much drinking and loud talking among the men, that it was thought best to send us children back to the camp.

It was at this place that we found many sand boulders like a big "white man's house." There were holes in them like rooms, and we played in these cave-like holes. One day, in the midst of our game, we found the skeleton of a great bear. Evidently he had been wounded and came there to die, for there were several arrows on the floor of the cave.

The most exciting event of this year was the attack that the Gros Ventres made upon us just as we moved our camp upon the table land back of the river in the spring. We had plenty of meat then and everybody was happy. The grass was beginning to appear and the ponies to grow fat.

One night there was a war dance. A few of our young men had planned to invade the Gros Ventres country, but it seemed that they too had been thinking of us. Everybody was interested in the proposed war party.

"Uncle, are you going too?" I eagerly asked him.

"No," he replied, with a long sigh. "It is the worst time of year to go on the war-path. We shall have plenty of fighting this summer, as we are going to trench upon their territory in our hunts," he added.

The night was clear and pleasant. The war drum was answered by the howls of coyotes on the opposite side of the Mouse river. I was in the throng, watching the braves who were about to go out in search of glory. "I wish I were old enough; I would surely go with this party," I thought. My friend Tatanka was to go. He was several years older than I, and a hero in my eyes. I watched him as he danced with the rest until nearly midnight. Then I came back to our teepee and rolled myself in my buffalo robe and was soon lost in sleep.

Suddenly I was aroused by loud war cries. "'Woo! woo! hay-ay! hay-ay! U we do! U we do!'" I jumped upon my feet, snatched my bow and arrows and rushed out of the teepee, frantically yelling as I went.

"Stop! stop!" screamed Uncheedah, and caught me by my long hair.

By this time the Gros Ventres had encircled our camp, sending volleys of arrows and bullets into our midst. The women were digging ditches in which to put their children.

My uncle was foremost in the battle. The Sioux bravely withstood the assault, although several of our men had already fallen. Many of the enemy were killed in the field around our teepees. The Sioux at last got their ponies and made a counter charge, led by Oyemakasan (my uncle). They cut the Gros Ventre party in two, and drove them off.

My friend Tatanka was killed. I took one of his eagle feathers, thinking I would wear it the first time that I ever went upon the war-path. I thought I would give anything for the opportunity to go against the Gros Ventres, because they killed my friend. The war songs, the wailing for the dead, the howling of the dogs was intolerable to me. Soon after this we broke up our camp and departed for new scenes.

III. Wild Harvests

WHEN OUR PEOPLE LIVED IN Minnesota, a good part of their natural subsistence was furnished by the wild rice, which grew abundantly in all of that region. Around the shores and all over some of the innumerable lakes of the "Land of Sky-blue Water" was this wild cereal found. Indeed, some of the watery fields in those days might be compared in extent and fruitfulness with the fields of wheat on Minnesota's magnificent farms today.

The wild rice harvesters came in groups of fifteen to twenty families to a lake, depending upon the size of the harvest. Some of the Indians hunted buffalo upon the prairie at this season, but there were more who preferred to go to the lakes to gather wild rice, fish, gather berries and hunt the deer. There was an abundance of water-fowls among the grain; and really no season of the year was happier than this.

The camping-ground was usually an attractive spot, with shade and cool breezes off the water. The people, while they pitched their teepees upon the heights, if possible, for the sake of a good outlook, actually lived in their canoes upon the placid waters. The happiest of all, perhaps, were the young maidens, who were all day long in their canoes, in twos or threes, and when tired of gathering the wild cereal, would sit in the boats doing their needle-work.

These maidens learned to imitate the calls of the different water-fowls as a sort of signal to the members of a group. Even the old women and the boys adopted signals, so that while the population of the village was lost to sight in a thick field of wild rice, a meeting could be arranged without calling any one by his or her own name. It was a great convenience for those young men who sought opportunity to meet certain maidens, for there were many canoe paths through the rice.

August is the harvest month. There were many preliminary feasts of fish, ducks and venison, and offerings in honor of the "Water Chief," so that there might not be any drowning accident during the harvest. The preparation consisted of a series of feasts and offerings for many days, while women and men were making birch canoes, for nearly every member of the family must be provided with one for this occasion. The blueberry and huckleberry-picking also preceded the rice-gathering.

There were social events which enlivened the camp of the harvesters; such as maidens' feasts, dances and a canoe regatta or two, in which not only the men were participants, but women and young girls as well.

On the appointed day all the canoes were carried to the shore and placed upon the water with prayer and propitiatory offerings. Each family took possession of the allotted field, and tied all the grain in bundles of convenient size, allowing it to stand for a few days. Then they again entered the lake, assigning two persons to each canoe. One manipulated the paddle, while the foremost one gently drew the heads of each bundle toward him and gave it a few strokes with a light rod. This caused the rice to fall into the bottom of the craft. The field was traversed in this manner back and forth until finished.

This was the pleasantest and easiest part of the harvest toil. The real work was when they prepared the rice for use. First of all, it must be made perfectly dry. They would spread it upon buffalo robes and mats, and sometimes upon layers of coarse swamp grass, and dry it in the sun. If the time was short, they would make a scaffold and spread upon it a certain thickness of the green grass and afterward the rice. Under this a fire was made, taking care that the grass did not catch fire.

When all the rice is gathered and dried, the hulling begins. A round hole is dug about two feet deep and the same in diameter. Then the rice is heated over a fire-place, and emptied into the hole while it is hot. A young man, having washed his feet and put on a new pair of moccasins, treads upon it until all is hulled. The women then pour it upon a robe and begin to shake it so that the chaff will be separated by the wind. Some of the rice is browned before being hulled.

During the hulling time there were prizes offered to the young men who can hull quickest and best. There were sometimes from twenty to fifty youths dancing with their feet in these holes.

Pretty moccasins were brought by shy maidens to the youths of their choice, asking them to hull rice. There were daily entertainments which deserved some such name as "hulling bee"—at any rate, we all enjoyed them hugely. The girls brought with them plenty of good things to eat.

When all the rice was prepared for the table, the matter of storing it must be determined. Caches were dug by each family in a concealed spot, and carefully lined with dry grass and bark. Here they left their surplus stores for a time of need. Our people were very ingenious in covering up all traces of the hidden food. A common trick was to build a fire on top of the mound. As much of the rice as could be carried conveniently was packed in par-fleches, or cases made of rawhide, and brought back with us to our village.

After all, the wild Indians could not be justly termed improvident, when their manner of life is taken into consideration. They let nothing go to waste, and labored incessantly during the summer and fall to lay up provision for the inclement season. Berries of all kinds were industriously gathered, and dried in the sun. Even the wild cherries were pounded up, stones and all, made into small cakes and dried for use in soups and for mixing with the pounded jerked meat and fat to form a much-prized Indian delicacy.

Out on the prairie in July and August the women were wont to dig teepsinna with sharpened sticks, and many a bag full was dried and put away. This teepsinna is the root of a certain plant growing mostly upon high sandy soil. It is starchy but solid, with a sweetish taste, and is very fattening. The fully grown teepsinna is two or three inches long, and has a dark-brown bark not unlike the bark of a young tree. It can be eaten raw or stewed, and is always kept in a dried state, except when it is first dug.

There was another root that our people gathered in small quantities. It is a wild sweet potato, found in bottom lands or river beds.

The primitive housekeeper exerted herself much to secure a variety of appetizing dishes; she even robbed the field mouse and the muskrat to accomplish her end. The tiny mouse gathers for her winter use several excellent kinds of food. Among these is a wild bean which equals in flavor any domestic bean that I have ever tasted. Her storehouse is usually under a peculiar mound, which the untrained eye would be unable to distinguish from an ant-hill. There are many pockets underneath, into which she industriously gathers the harvest of the summer.

She is fortunate if the quick eye of a native woman does not detect her hiding-place. About the month of September, while traveling over the prairie, a woman is occasionally observed to halt suddenly and waltz around a suspected mound. Finally the pressure of her heel causes a place to give way, and she settles contentedly down to rob the poor mouse of the fruits of her labor.

The different kinds of beans are put away in different pockets, but it is the oomenechah she wants. The field mouse loves this savory vegetable, for she always gathers it more than any other. There is also some of the white star-like manakcahkcah, the root of the wild lily. This is a good medicine and good to eat.

When our people were gathering the wild rice, they always watched for another plant that grows in the muddy bottom of lakes and ponds. It is a white bulb about the size of an ordinary onion. This is stored away by the muskrats in their houses by the waterside, and there is often a bushel or more of the psinchinchah to be found within. It seemed as if everybody was good to the wild Indian; at least we thought so then.

I have referred to the opportunities for courting upon the wild rice fields. Indian courtship is very peculiar in many respects; but when you study their daily life you will see the philosophy of their etiquette of love-making. There was no parlor courtship; the life was largely out-of-doors, which was very favorable to the young men

In a nomadic life where the female members of the family have entire control of domestic affairs, the work is divided among them all. Very often the bringing of the wood and water devolves upon the young maids, and the spring or the woods become the battle-ground of love's warfare. The nearest water may be some distance from the camp, which is all the better. Sometimes, too, there is no wood to be had; and in that case, one would see the young women scattered all over the prairie, gathering buffalo chips for fuel.

This is the way the red men go about to induce the aboriginal maids to listen to their suit. As soon as the youth has returned from the war-path or the chase, he puts on his porcupine-quill embroidered moccasins and leggings, and folds his best robe about him. He brushes his long, glossy hair with a brush made from the tail of the porcupine, perfumes it with scented grass or leaves, then arranges it in two plaits with an otter skin or some other ornament. If he is a warrior, he adds an eagle feather or two.

If he chooses to ride, he takes his best pony. He jumps upon its bare back, simply throwing a part of his robe under him to serve as a saddle, and holding the end of a lariat tied about the animal's neck. He guides him altogether by the motions of his body. These wily ponies seem to enter into the spirit of the occasion, and very often capture the eyes of the maid by their graceful movements, in perfect obedience to their master.

The general custom is for the young men to pull their robes over their heads, leaving only a slit to look through. Sometimes the same is done by the maiden—especially in public courtship.

He approaches the girl while she is coming from the spring. He takes up his position directly in her path. If she is in a hurry or does not care to stop, she goes around him; but if she is willing to stop and listen she puts down on the ground the vessel of water she is carrying.

Very often at the first meeting the maiden does not know who her lover is. He does not introduce himself immediately, but waits until a second meeting. Sometimes she does not see his face at all; and then she will try to find out who he is and what he looks like before they meet again. If he is not a desirable suitor, she will go with her chaperon and end the affair there.

There are times when maidens go in twos, and then there must be two young men to meet them.

There is some courtship in the night time; either in the early part of the evening, on the outskirts of dances and other public affairs, or after everybody is supposed to be asleep. This is the secret courtship. The youth may pull up the tentpins just back of his sweetheart and speak with her during the night. He must be a smart young man to do that undetected, for the grandmother, her chaperon, is usually "all ears."

Elopements are common. There are many reasons for a girl or a youth to defer their wedding. It may be from personal pride of one or both. The well-born are married publicly, and many things are given away in their honor. The maiden may desire to attend a certain number of maidens' feasts before marrying. The youth may be poor, or he may wish to achieve another honor before surrendering to a woman.

Sometimes a youth is so infatuated with a maiden that he will follow her to any part of the country, even after their respective bands have separated for the season. I knew of one such case. Patah Tankah had courted a distant relative of my uncle for a long time. There seemed to be some objection to him on the part of the girl's parents, although the girl herself was willing.

The large camp had been broken up for the fall hunt, and my uncle's band went one way, while the young man's family went in the other direction. After three days' travelling, we came to a good hunting-ground, and made camp. One evening somebody saw the young man. He had been following his sweetheart and sleeping out-of-doors all that time, although the nights were already frosty and cold. He met her every day in secret and she brought him food, but he would not come near the teepee. Finally her people yielded, and she went back with him to his band.

When we lived our natural life, there was much singing of war songs, medicine, hunting and love songs. Sometimes there were few words or none, but everything was understood by the inflection. From this I have often thought that there must be a language of dumb beasts.

The crude musical instrument of the Sioux, the flute, was made to appeal to the susceptible ears of the maidens late into the night. There comes to me now the picture of two young men with their robes over their heads, and only a portion of the hand-made and carved chotanka, the flute, protruding from its folds. I can see all the maidens slyly turn their heads to listen. Now I hear one of the youths begin to sing a plaintive serenade as in days gone by:

> *"Hay-ay-ay! Hay-ay-ay! a-ahay-ay!" (This*
> *"Listen! you will hear of him—*
> *Maiden, you will hear of him—*
> *Listen! he will shortly go*

Wasula feels that she must come out, but she has no good excuse, so she stirs up the embers of the fire and causes an unnecessary smoke in the teepee. Then she has an excuse to come out and fix up the tent flaps. She takes a long time to adjust these pointed ears of the teepee, with their long poles, for the wind seems to be unsettled.

Finally Chotanka ceases to be heard. In a moment a young man appears ghost-like at the maiden's side.

"So it is you, is it?" she asks.

"Is your grandmother in?" he inquires.

"What a brave man you are, to fear an old woman! We are free; the country is wide. We can go away, and come back when the storm is over."

"Ho," he replies. "It is not that I fear her, or the consequences of an elopement. I fear nothing except that we may be separated!"

The girl goes into the lodge for a moment, then slips out once more. "Now," she exclaims, "to the wood or the prairie! I am yours!" They disappear in the darkness.

IV. A Meeting on the Plains

WE WERE ENCAMPED AT ONE time on the Souris or Mouse river, a tributary of the Assiniboine. The buffaloes were still plenty; hence we were living on the "fat of the land." One afternoon a scout came in with the announcement that a body of United States troops was approaching! This report, of course, caused much uneasiness among our people.

A council was held immediately, in the course of which the scout was put through a rigid examination. Before a decision had been reached, another scout came in from the field. He declared that the moving train reported as a body of troops was in reality a train of Canadian carts.

The two reports differed so widely that it was deemed wise to send out more runners to observe this moving body closely, and ascertain definitely its character. These soon returned with the positive information that the Canadians were at hand, "for," said they, "there are no bright metals in the moving train to send forth flashes of light. The separate bodies are short, like carts with ponies, and not like the long, four-wheeled wagon drawn by four or six mules, that the soldiers use. They are not buffaloes, and they cannot be mounted troops, with pack-mules, because the individual bodies are too long for that. Besides, the soldiers usually have their chief, with his guards, leading the train; and the little chiefs are also separated from the main body and ride at one side!"

From these observations it was concluded that we were soon to meet with the bois brules, as the French call their mixed-bloods, presumably from the color of their complexions. Some say that they are named from the "burned forests" which, as wood-cutters, they are accustomed to leave behind them. Two or three hours later, at about sunset, our ears began to distinguish the peculiar music that always accompanied a moving train of their carts. It is like the grunting and squealing of many animals, and is due to the fact that the wheels and all other parts of these vehicles are made of wood. Our dogs gleefully augmented the volume of inharmonious sound.

They stopped a little way from our camp, upon a grassy plain, and the ponies were made to wheel their clumsy burdens into a perfect circle, the shafts being turned inward. Thus was formed a sort of barricade—quite a usual and necessary precaution in their nomadic and adventurous life. Within this circle the tents were pitched, and many cheerful fires were soon kindled. The garcons were hurriedly driving the ponies to water, with much cracking of whips and outbursting of impatient oaths.

Our chief and his principal warriors briefly conferred with the strangers, and it was understood by both parties that no thought of hostilities lurked in the minds of either.

After having observed the exchange of presents that always follows a "peace council," there were friendly and hospitable feasts in both camps. The bois brules had been long away from any fort or trading-post, and it so happened that their inevitable whiskey keg was almost empty. They had diluted the few gills remaining with several large kettles full of water. In order to have any sort of offensive taste, it was necessary to add cayenne pepper and a little gentian.

Our men were treated to this concoction; and seeing that two or three of the half-breeds pretended to become intoxicated, our braves followed their example. They made night intolerable with their shouts and singing until past midnight, when gradually all disturbance ceased, and both camps appeared to be wrapped in deep slumber.

Suddenly the loud report of a gun stirred the sleepers. Many more reports were heard in quick succession, all coming from the camp of the bois brules. Every man among the Sioux sprang to his feet, weapon in hand, and many ran towards their ponies. But there was one significant point about the untimely firing of the guns—they were all directed heavenward! One of our old men, who understood better than any one else the manners of the half-breeds, thus proclaimed at the top of his voice:

"Let the people sleep! This that we have heard is the announcement of a boy's advent into the world! It is their custom to introduce with gunpowder a new-born boy!"

Again quiet was restored in the neighboring camps, and for a time the night reigned undisturbed. But scarcely had we fallen into a sound sleep when we were for the second time rudely aroused by the firing of guns and the yelling of warriors. This time it was discovered that almost all the ponies, including those of our neighbors, had been stealthily driven off by horse-thieves of another tribe.

These miscreants were adepts in their profession, for they had accomplished their purpose with much skill, almost under the very eyes of the foe, and had it not been for the invincible superstition of Slow Dog, they would have met with complete success. As it was, they caused us no little trouble and anxiety, but after a hot pursuit of a whole day, with the assistance of the halfbreeds our horses were recaptured.

Slow Dog was one of those Indians who are filled with conceit, and boasting loudly their pretensions as medicine men, without any success, only bring upon themselves an unnecessary amount of embarrassment and ridicule. Yet there is one quality always possessed by such persons, among a savage people as elsewhere—namely, great perseverance and tenacity in their self-assertion. So the blessing of ignorance kept Slow Dog always cheerful; and he seemed, if anything, to derive some pleasure from the endless insinuations and ridicule of the people!

Now Slow Dog had loudly proclaimed, on the night before this event, that he had received the warning of a bad dream, in which he had seen all the ponies belonging to the tribe stampeded and driven westward.

"But who cares for Slow Dog's dream?" said everybody; "none of the really great medicine men have had any such visions!"

Therefore our little community, given as they were to superstition, anticipated no special danger. It is true that when the first scout reported the approach of troops some of the people had weakened, and said to one another:

"After all, perhaps poor Slow Dog may be right; but we are always too ready to laugh at him!"

However, this feeling quickly passed away when the jovial Canadians arrived, and the old man was left alone to brood upon his warning.

He was faithful to his dream. During all the hilarity of the feast and the drinking of the mock whiskey, be acted as self-constituted sentinel. Finally, when everybody else had succumbed to sleep, he gathered together several broken and discarded lariats of various materials—leather, buffalo's hair and horse's hair. Having lengthened this variegated rope with innumerable knots, he fastened one end of it around the neck of his old war-horse, and tied the other to his wrist. Instead of sleeping inside the tent as usual, he rolled himself in a buffalo robe and lay down in its shadow. From this place he watched until the moon had disappeared behind the western horizon; and just as the grey dawn began to appear in the east his eyes were attracted to what seemed to be a dog moving among the picketed ponies. Upon a closer scrutiny, he saw that its actions were unnatural.

"Toka abe do! toka abe do!" (the enemy! the enemy!) exclaimed Slow Dog. With a warwhoop he sprang toward the intruder, who rose up and leaped upon the back of Slow Dog's warsteed. He had cut the hobble, as well as the device of the old medicine man.

The Sioux now bent his bow to shoot, but it was too late. The other quickly dodged behind the animal, and from under its chest he sent a deadly arrow to Slow Dog's bosom. Then he remounted the pony and set off at full speed after his comrades, who had already started.

As the Sioux braves responded to the alarm, and passed by the daring old warrior in pursuit of their enemies, who had stampeded most of the loose ponies, the old man cried out:

"I, brave Slow Dog, who have so often made a path for you on the field of battle, am now about to make one to the land of spirits!"

So speaking, the old man died. The Sioux were joined in the chase by the friendly mixedbloods, and in the end the Blackfeet were compelled to pay dearly for the blood of the poor old man.

On that beautiful morning all Nature seemed brilliant and smiling, but the Sioux were mourning and wailing for the death of one who had been an object of ridicule during most of his life. They appreciated the part that Slow Dog had played in this last event, and his memory was honored by all the tribe.

V. An Adventurous Journey

IT MUST NOW BE ABOUT thirty years since our long journey in search of new hunting-grounds, from the Assiniboine river to the Upper Missouri. The buffalo, formerly so abundant between the two rivers, had begun to shun their usual haunts, on account of the great numbers of Canadian halfbreeds in that part of the country. There was also the first influx of English sportsmen, whose wholesale methods of destruction wrought such havoc with the herds. These seemingly intelligent animals correctly prophesied to the natives the approach of the pale-face.

As we had anticipated, we found game very scarce as we travelled slowly across the vast plains. There were only herds of antelope and sometimes flocks of waterfowl, with here and there a lonely bull straggling aimlessly along. At first our party was small, but as we proceeded on our way we fell in with some of the western bands of Sioux and Assiniboines, who are close connections.

Each day the camp was raised and marched from ten to twenty miles. One might wonder how such a cavalcade would look in motion. The only vehicles were the primitive travaux drawn by ponies and large Esquimaux dogs. These are merely a pair of shafts fastened on either side of the animal, and trailing on the ground behind. A large basket suspended between the poles, just above the ground, supplied a place for goods and a safe nest for the babies, or an occasional helpless old woman. Most of our effects were carried by pack ponies; and an Indian packer excels all others in quickness and dexterity.

The train was nearly a mile long, headed by a number of old warriors on foot, who carried the filled pipe, and decided when and where to stop. A very warm day made much trouble for the women who had charge of the moving household. The pack dogs were especially unmanageable. They would become very thirsty and run into the water with their loads. The scolding of the women, the singing of the old men and the yelps of the Indian dudes made our progress a noisy one, and like that of a town in motion rather than an ordinary company of travelers.

This journey of ours was not without its exciting episodes. My uncle had left the main body and gone off to the south with a small party, as he was accustomed to do every summer, to seek revenge of some sort on the whites for all the injuries that they had inflicted upon our family. This time he met with a company of soldiers between Fort Totten and Fort Berthold, in North Dakota. Somehow, these seven Indians surprised the troopers in broad daylight, while eating their dinner, and captured the whole outfit, including nearly all their mules and one white horse, with such of their provisions as they cared to carry back with them. No doubt these soldiers reported at the fort that they had been attacked by a large party of Indians, and I dare say some promotions rewarded their tale of a brave defense! However, the facts are just as I have stated them. My uncle brought home the white horse, and the fine Spanish mules were taken by the others. Among the things they brought back with them were several loaves of raised bread, the first I had ever seen, and a great curiosity. We called it aguyape tachangu, or lung bread, from its spongy consistency.

Although when a successful war-party returns with so many trophies, there is usually much dancing and hilarity, there was almost nothing of the kind on this occasion. The reason was that the enemy made little resistance; and then there was our old tradition with regard to the whites that there is no honor in conquering them, as they fight only under compulsion. Had there really been a battle, and some of our men been killed, there would have been some enthusiasm.

It was upon this journey that a hunter performed the feat of shooting an arrow through three antelopes. This statement may perhaps be doubted, yet I can vouch for its authenticity. He was not alone at the time, and those who were with him are reliable witnesses. The animals were driven upon a marshy peninsula, where they were crowded together and almost helpless. Many were despatched with knives and arrows; and a man by the name of Grey-foot, who was large and tall and an extraordinarily fine hunter, actually sent his arrow through three of them. This feat was not accomplished by mere strength, for it requires a great deal of skill as well.

A misfortune occurred near the river which deprived us of one of our best young men. There was no other man, except my own uncle, for whom I had at that time so great an admiration. Very strangely, as it appeared to me, he bore a Christian name. He was commonly called Jacob. I did not discover how he came by such a curious and apparently meaningless name until after I had returned to the United States. His father had been converted by one of the early missionaries, before the

Minnesota massacre in 1862, and the boy had been baptized Jacob. He was an ideal woodsman and hunter and really a hero in my eyes. He was one of the party of seven who had attacked and put to rout the white soldiers.

The trouble arose thus. Jacob had taken from the soldiers two good mules, and soon afterward we fell in with some Canadian half-breeds who were desirous of trading for them. However, the young man would not trade; he was not at all disposed to part with his fine mules. A certain one of the mixed-bloods was intent upon getting possession of these animals by fair or unfair means. He invited Jacob to dinner, and treated him to whiskey; but the Indian youth declined the liquor. The half-breed pretended to take this refusal to drink as an insult. He seized his gun and shot his guest dead.

In a few minutes the scene was one of almost unprecedented excitement. Every adult Indian, female as well as male, was bent upon invading the camp of the bois brules, to destroy the murderer. The confusion was made yet more intolerable by the wailing of the women and the singing of death-songs.

Our number was now ten to one of the halfbreeds. Within the circle formed by their carts they prepared for a desperate resistance. The hills about their little encampment were covered with warriors, ready to pounce upon them at the signal of their chief.

The older men, however, were discussing in council what should be demanded of the halfbreeds. It was determined that the murderer must be given up to us, to be punished according to the laws of the plains. If, however, they should refuse to give him up, the mode of attack decided upon was to build a fire around the offenders and thus stampede their horses, or at the least divide their attention. Meanwhile, the braves were to make a sudden onset.

Just then a piece of white, newly-tanned deerskin was hoisted up in the center of the bois brule encampment. It was a flag of truce. One of their number approached the council lodge, unarmed and making the sign for a peaceful communication. He was admitted to the council, which was still in session, and offered to give up the murderer. It was also proposed, as an alternative, that he be compelled to give everything he had to the parents of the murdered man.

The parents were allowed no voice whatever in the discussion which followed, for they were regarded as incompetent judges, under the circumstances. It was finally decreed by the council that the man's life should be spared, but that he must be exposed to the indignity of a public whipping, and resign all his earthly possessions to the parents of his victim. This sentence was carried into effect.

In our nomadic life there were a few unwritten laws by which our people were governed. There was a council, a police force, and an executive officer, who was not always the chief, but a member of the tribe appointed to this position for a given number of days. There were also the wise old men who were constantly in attendance at the council lodge, and acted as judges in the rare event of the commission of a crime.

This simple government of ours was supported by the issue of little sticks about five inches long. There were a hundred or so of these, and they were distributed every few days by the police or soldiers, who kept account of them. Whoever received one of these sticks must return it within five or ten days, with a load of provisions. If one was held beyond the stipulated time the police would call the delinquent warrior to account. In case he did not respond, they could come and destroy his tent or take away his weapons. When all the sticks had been returned, they were reissued to other men; and so the council lodge was supported.

It was the custom that no man who had not distinguished himself upon the war-path could destroy the home of another. This was a necessary qualification for the office of an Indian policeman. These policemen must also oversee the hunt, lest some individuals should be well provided with food while others were in want. No man might hunt independently. The game must be carefully watched by the game scouts, and the discovery of a herd reported at once to the council, after which the time and manner of the hunt were publicly announced.

I well recall how the herald announced the near approach of buffaloes. It was supposed that if the little boys could trip up the old man while going his rounds, the success of the hunt was assured. The oftener he was tripped, the more successful it would be! The signal or call for buffaloes was a peculiar whistle. As soon as the herald appeared, all the boys would give the whistle and follow in crowds after the poor old man. Of course he tried to avoid them, but they were generally too quick for him.

There were two kinds of scouts, for hunting and for war. In one sense every Indian was a scout; but there were some especially appointed to serve for a certain length of time. An Indian might hunt every day, besides the regularly organized hunt; but he was liable to punishment at any time. If he could kill a solitary buffalo or deer without disturbing the herd, it was allowed. He might also hunt small game.

In the movable town under such a government as this, there was apt to be inconvenience and actual suffering, since a great body of people were supported only by the daily hunt. Hence there was a constant disposition to break up into smaller parties, in order to obtain food more easily and freely. Yet the wise men of the Dakotas would occasionally form large bands of from two to five thousand people, who camped and moved about together for a period of some months. It is apparent that so large a body could not be easily supplied with the necessaries of life; but, on the other hand, our enemies respected such a gathering! Of course the nomadic government would do its utmost to hold together as long as possible. The police did all they could to keep in check those parties who were intent upon stealing away.

There were many times, however, when individual bands and even families were justified in seeking to separate themselves from the rest, in order to gain a better support. It was chiefly by reason of this food question that the Indians never established permanent towns or organized themselves into a more formidable nation.

There was a sad misfortune which, although it happened many generations ago, was familiarly quoted among us. A certain band became very independent and unruly; they went so far as to wilfully disobey the orders of the general government. The police were directed to punish the leader severely; whereupon the rest defended him and resisted the police. But the latter were competent to enforce their authority, and as a result the entire band was annihilated.

One day, as we were following along the bank of the Upper Missouri, there appeared to be a great disturbance at the head of the cavalcade—so much so that we thought our people had been attacked by a war-party of the Crows or some of the hostile tribes of that region. In spite of the danger, even the women and children hurried forward to join the men—that is to say, as many as were not upon the hunt. Most of the warriors were out, as usual, and only the large boys and the old men were travelling with the women and their domestic effects and little ones.

As we approached the scene of action, we heard loud shouts and the report of fire-arms; but our party was scattered along for a considerable distance, and all was over before we could reach the spot. It was a great grizzly bear who had been bold enough to oppose, single-handed, the progress of several hundred Indians. The council-men, who usually walked a little in advance of the train, were the first to meet the bear, and he was probably deceived by the sight of this advance body, and thus audaciously defied them.

Among these council-men—all retired chiefs and warriors whose ardent zeal for the display of courage had long been cooled, and whose present duties were those of calm deliberation for their people's welfare—there were two old, distinguished war-chiefs. Each of these men still carried his war-lance, wrapped up in decorated buckskin. As the bear advanced boldly toward them, the two old men promptly threw off their robes—an evidence that there still lurked within their breasts the spirit of chivalry and ready courage. Spear in hand, they both sprang forward to combat with the ferocious animal, taking up their positions about ten feet apart.

As they had expected, the fearful beast, after getting up on his haunches and growling savagely, came forward with widely opened jaws. He fixed his eyes upon the left-hand man, who was ready to meet him with uplifted spear, but with one stroke of his powerful paw the weapon was sent to the ground. At the same moment the right-hand man dealt him a stab that penetrated the grizzly's side.

The bear uttered a groan not unlike that of a man, and seized the spear so violently that its owner was thrown to the ground. As the animal drew the lance from its body, the first man, having recovered his own, stabbed him with it on the other side. Upon this, he turned and knocked the old man down, and again endeavored to extract the spear.

By this time all the dogs and men were at hand. Many arrows and balls were sent into the tough hide of the bear. Yet he would probably have killed both his assailants, had it not been for the active small dogs who were constantly upon his heels and annoying him. A deadly rifle shot at last brought him down.

The old men were badly bruised and torn, but both of them recovered, to bear from that day the high-sounding titles of "Fought-the-Bear" and "Conquered-the-Grizzly."

XI

The Laughing Philosopher

There is scarcely anything so exasperating to me as the idea that the natives of this country have no sense of humor and no faculty for mirth. This phase of their character is well understood by those whose fortune or misfortune it has been to live among them day in and day out at their homes. I don't believe I ever heard a real hearty laugh away from the Indians' fireside. I have often spent an entire evening in laughing with them until I could laugh no more. There are evenings when the recognized wit or story-teller of the village gives a free entertainment which keeps the rest of the community in a convulsive state until he leaves them. However, Indian humor consists as much in the gestures and inflections of the voice as in words, and is really untranslatable.

Matogee (Yellow Bear) was a natural humorous speaker, and a very diffident man at other times. He usually said little, but when he was in the mood he could keep a large company in a roar. This was especially the case whenever he met his brother-in-law, Tamedokah.

It was a custom with us Indians to joke more particularly with our brothers- and sisters-in-law. But no one ever complained, or resented any of these jokes, however personal they might be. That would be an unpardonable breach of etiquette.

"Tamedokah, I heard that you tried to capture a buck by holding on to his tail," said Matogee, laughing. "I believe that feat cannot be performed any more; at least, it never has been since the pale-face brought us the knife, the 'mysterious iron,' and the pulverized coal that makes bullets fly. Since our ancestors hunted with stone knives and hatchets, I say, that has never been done."

The fact was that Tamedokah had stunned a buck that day while hunting, and as he was about to dress him the animal got up and attempted to run, whereupon the Indian launched forth to secure his game. He only succeeded in grasping the tail of the deer, and was pulled about all over the meadows and the adjacent woods until the tail came off in his hands. Matogee thought this too good a joke to be lost.

I sat near the door of the tent, and thoroughly enjoyed the story of the comical accident.

"Yes," Tamedokah quietly replied, "I thought I would do something to beat the story of the man who rode a young elk, and yelled frantically for help, crying like a woman."

"Ugh! that was only a legend," retorted Matogee, for it was he who was the hero of this tale in his younger days. "But this is a fresh feat of today. Chankpayuhah said he could not tell which was the most scared, the buck or you," he continued. "He said the deer's eyes were bulging out of their sockets, while Tamedokah's mouth was constantly enlarging toward his ears, and his hair floated on the wind, shaking among the branches of the trees. That will go down with the traditions of our fathers," he concluded with an air of satisfaction.

"It was a singular mishap," admitted Tamedokah.

The pipe had been filled by Matogee and passed to Tamedokah good-naturedly, still with a broad smile on his face. "It must be acknowledged," he resumed, "that you have the strongest kind of a grip, for no one else could hold on as long as you did, and secure such a trophy besides. That tail will do for an eagle feather holder."

By this time the teepee was packed to overflowing. Loud laughter had been heard issuing from the lodge of Matogee, and everybody suspected that he had something good, so many had come to listen.

"I think we should hear the whole matter," said one of the late comers.

The teepee was brightly lit by the burning embers, and all the men were sitting with their knees up against their chests, held in that position by wrapping their robes tightly around loins and knees. This fixed them something in the fashion of a rocking-chair.

"Well, no one saw him except Chankpayuhah," Matogee remarked.

"Yes, yes, he must tell us about it," exclaimed a chorus of voices.

"This is what I saw," the witness began. "I was tracking a buck and a doe. As I approached a small opening at the creek side 'boom!' came a report of the mysterious iron. I remained in a stooping position, hoping to see a deer cross the opening. In this I was not disappointed, for immediately after the report a fine buck dashed forth with Tamedokah close behind him. The latter was holding on to the deer's tail with both hands and his knife was in his mouth, but it soon dropped out. 'Tamedokah,' I shouted, 'haven't you got hold of the wrong animal?' but as I spoke they disappeared into the woods.

"In a minute they both appeared again, and then it was that I began to laugh. I could not stop. It almost killed me. The deer jumped the longest jumps I ever saw. Tamedokah walked the longest paces and was very swift. His hair was whipping the trees as they went by. Water poured down his face. I stood bent forward because I could not straighten my back-bone, and was ready to fall when they again disappeared.

"When they came out for the third time it seemed as if the woods and the meadow were moving too. Tamedokah skipped across the opening as if he were a grasshopper learning to hop. I fell down.

"When I came to he was putting water on my face and head, but when I looked at him I fell again, and did not know anything until the sun had passed the mid-sky.

"The company was kept roaring all the way through this account, while Tamedokah himself heartily joined in the mirth.

"Ho, ho, ho!" they said; "he has made his name famous in our annals. This will be told of him henceforth."

"It reminds me of Chadozee's bear story," said one.

"His was more thrilling, because it was really dangerous," interposed another.

"You can tell it to us, Bobdoo," remarked a third.

The man thus addressed made no immediate reply. He was smoking contentedly. At last he silently returned the pipe to Matogee, with whom it had begun its rounds. Deliberately he tightened his robe around him, saying as he did so:

"Ho (Yes). I was with him. It was by a very little that he saved his life. I will tell you how it happened.

"I was hunting with these two men, Nageedah and Chadozee. We came to some wild cherry bushes. I began to eat of the fruit when I saw a large silver-tip crawling toward us. 'Look out! there is a grizzly here,' I shouted, and I ran my pony out on to the prairie; but the others had already dismounted.

"Nageedah had just time to jump upon his pony and get out of the way, but the bear seized hold of his robe and pulled it off. Chadozee stood upon the verge of a steep bank, below which there ran a deep and swift-flowing stream. The bear rushed upon him so suddenly that when he took a step backward, they both fell into the creek together. It was a fall of about twice the height of a man."

"Did they go out of sight?" some one inquired.

"Yes, both fell headlong. In his excitement Chadozee laid hold of the bear in the water, and I never saw a bear try so hard to get away from a man as this one did."

"Ha, ha, ha! ha, ha, ha!" they all laughed.

"When they came to the surface again they were both so eager to get to the shore that each let go, and they swam as quickly as they could to opposite sides. Chadozee could not get any further, so he clung to a stray root, still keeping a close watch of the bear, who was forced to do the same. There they both hung, regarding each other with looks of contempt and defiance."

"Ha, ha, ha! ha, ha, ha!" they all laughed again.

"At last the bear swam along the edge to a lower place, and we pulled Chadozee up by means of our lariats. All this time he had been groaning so loud that we supposed he was badly torn; but when I looked for his wounds I found a mere scratch."

Again the chorus of appreciation from his hearers.

"The strangest thing about this affair of mine," spoke up Tamedokah, "is that I dreamed the whole thing the night before."

"There are some dreams come true, and I am a believer in dreams," one remarked.

"Yes, certainly, so are we all. You know Hachah almost lost his life by believing in dreams," commented Matogee.

"Let us hear that story," was the general request.

"You have all heard of Hachah, the great medicine man, who did many wonderful things. He once dreamed four nights in succession of flying from a high cliff over the Minnesota river. He recollected every particular of the scene, and it made a great impression upon his mind.

"The next day after he had dreamed it for the fourth time, he proposed to his wife that they go down to the river to swim, but his real purpose was to see the place of his dream.

"He did find the place, and it seemed to Hachah exactly like. A crooked tree grew out of the top of the cliff, and the water below was very deep."

"Did he really fly?" I called impatiently from the doorway, where I had been listening and laughing with the rest.

"Ugh, that is what I shall tell you. He was swimming about with his wife, who was a fine swimmer; but all at once Hachah disappeared. Presently he stood upon the very tree that he had seen in his dream, and gazed out over the water. The tree was very springy, and Hachah felt sure that he could fly; so before long he launched bravely forth from the cliff. He kicked out vigorously and swung both arms as he did so, but nevertheless he came down to the bottom of the water like a crow that had been shot on the wing."

"Ho, ho, ho! Ho, ho, ho!" and the whole company laughed unreservedly.

"His wife screamed loudly as Hachah whirled downward and went out of sight like a blue heron after a fish. Then she feared he might be stunned, so she swam to him and dragged him to the shore. He could not speak, but the woman overwhelmed him with reproaches.

"'What are you trying to do, you old idiot? Do you want to kill yourself?' she screamed again and again.

"'Woman, be silent,' he replied, and he said nothing more. He did not tell his dream for many years afterward. Not until he was a very old man and about to die, did Hachah tell any one how he thought he could fly."

And at this they all laughed louder than ever.

XII

First Impressions of Civilization

I was scarcely old enough to know anything definite about the "Big Knives," as we called the white men, when the terrible Minnesota massacre broke up our home and I was carried into exile. I have already told how I was adopted into the family of my father's younger brother, when my father was betrayed and imprisoned. We all supposed that he had shared the fate of those who were executed at Mankato, Minnesota.

Now the savage philosophers looked upon vengeance in the field of battle as a lofty virtue. To avenge the death of a relative or of a dear friend was considered a great deed. My uncle, accordingly, had spared no pains to instill into my young mind the obligation to avenge the death of my father and my older brothers. Already I looked eagerly forward to the day when I should find an opportunity to carry out his teachings. Meanwhile, he himself went upon the war-path and returned with scalps every summer. So it may be imagined how I felt toward the Big Knives!

On the other hand, I had heard marvelous things of this people. In some things we despised them; in others we regarded them as wakan (mysterious), a race whose power bordered upon the supernatural. I learned that they had made a "fireboat." I could not understand how they could unite two elements which cannot exist together. I thought the water would put out the fire, and the fire would consume the boat if it had the shadow of a chance. This was to me a preposterous thing! But when I was told that the Big Knives had created a "fire-boat-walks-on-mountains" (a locomotive) it was too much to believe.

"Why," declared my informant, "those who saw this monster move said that it flew from mountain to mountain when it seemed to be excited. They said also that they believed it carried a thunder-bird, for they frequently heard his usual war-whoop as the creature sped along!"

Several warriors had observed from a distance one of the first trains on the Northern Pacific, and had gained an exaggerated impression of the wonders of the pale-face. They had seen it go over a bridge that spanned a deep ravine and it seemed to them that it jumped from one bank to the other. I confess that the story almost quenched my ardor and bravery.

Two or three young men were talking together about this fearful invention.

"However," said one, "I understand that this fire-boat-walks-on-mountains cannot move except on the track made for it."

Although a boy is not expected to join in the conversation of his elders, I ventured to ask: "Then it cannot chase us into any rough country?"

"No, it cannot do that," was the reply, which I heard with a great deal of relief.

I had seen guns and various other things brought to us by the French Canadians, so that I had already some notion of the supernatural gifts of the white man; but I had never before heard such tales as I listened to that morning. It was said that they had bridged the Missouri and Mississippi rivers, and that they made immense houses of stone and brick, piled on top of one another until they were as high as high hills. My brain was puzzled with these things for many a day. Finally I asked my uncle why the Great Mystery gave such power to the Washechu (the rich)-sometimes we called them by this name—and not to us Dakotas.

"For the same reason," he answered, "that he gave to Duta the skill to make fine bows and arrows, and to Wachesne no skill to make anything."

"And why do the Big Knives increase so much more in number than the Dakotas?" I continued.

"It has been said, and I think it must be true, that they have larger families than we do. I went into the house of an Eashecha (a German), and I counted no less than nine children. The eldest of them could not have been over fifteen. When my grandfather first visited them, down at the mouth of the Mississippi, they were comparatively few; later my father visited their Great Father at Washington, and they had already spread over the whole country."

"Certainly they are a heartless nation. They have made some of their people servants—yes, slaves! We have never believed in keeping slaves, but it seems that these Washechu do! It is our belief that they painted their servants black a long time ago, to tell them from the rest, and now the slaves have children born to them of the same color!

"The greatest object of their lives seems to be to acquire possessions—to be rich. They desire to possess the whole world. For thirty years they were trying to entice us to sell them our land. Finally the outbreak gave them all, and we have been driven away from our beautiful country.

"They are a wonderful people. They have divided the day into hours, like the moons of the year. In fact, they measure everything. Not one of them would let so much as a turnip go from his field unless he received full value for it. I understand that their great men make a feast and invite many, but when the feast is over the guests are required to pay for what they have eaten before leaving the house. I myself saw at White Cliff (the name given to St. Paul, Minnesota) a man who kept a brass drum and a bell to call people to his table; but when he got them in he would make them pay for the food!

"I am also informed," said my uncle, "but this I hardly believe, that their Great Chief (President) compels every man to pay him for the land he lives upon and all his personal goods—even for his own existence—every year!" (This was his idea of taxation.) "I am sure we could not live under such a law.

"When the outbreak occurred, we thought that our opportunity had come, for we had learned that the Big Knives were fighting among themselves, on account of a dispute over their slaves. It was said that the Great Chief had allowed slaves in one part of the country and not in another, so there was jealousy, and they had to fight it out. We don't know how true this was.

"There were some praying-men who came to us some time before the trouble arose. They observed every seventh day as a holy day. On that day they met in a house that they had built for that purpose, to sing, pray, and speak of their Great Mystery. I was never in one of these meetings. I understand that they had a large book from which they read. By all accounts they were very different from all other white men we have known, for these never observed any such day, and we never knew them to pray, neither did they ever tell us of their Great Mystery.

"In war they have leaders and war-chiefs of different grades. The common warriors are driven forward like a herd of antelopes to face the foe. It is on account of this manner of fighting—from compulsion and not from personal bravery—that we count no coup on them. A lone warrior can do much harm to a large army of them in a bad country."

It was this talk with my uncle that gave me my first clear idea of the white man.

I was almost fifteen years old when my uncle presented me with a flint-lock gun. The possession of the "mysterious iron," and the explosive dirt, or "pulverized coal," as it is called, filled me with new thoughts. All the war-songs that I had ever heard from childhood came back to me with their heroes. It seemed as if I were an entirely new being—the boy had become a man!

"I am now old enough," said I to myself, "and I must beg my uncle to take me with him on his next war-path. I shall soon be able to go among the whites whenever I wish, and to avenge the blood of my father and my brothers."

I had already begun to invoke the blessing of the Great Mystery. Scarcely a day passed that I did not offer up some of my game, so that he might not be displeased with me. My people saw very little of me during the day, for in solitude I found the strength I needed. I groped about in the wilderness, and determined to assume my position as a man. My boyish ways were departing, and a sullen dignity and composure was taking their place.

The thought of love did not hinder my ambitions. I had a vague dream of some day courting a pretty maiden, after I had made my reputation, and won the eagle feathers.

One day, when I was away on the daily hunt, two strangers from the United States visited our camp. They had boldly ventured across the northern border. They were Indians, but clad in the white man's garments. It was as well that I was absent with my gun.

My father, accompanied by an Indian guide, after many days' searching had found us at last. He had been imprisoned at Davenport, Iowa, with those who took part in the massacre or in the battles following, and he was taught in prison and converted by the pioneer missionaries, Drs. Williamson and Riggs. He was under sentence of death, but was among the number against whom no direct evidence was found, and who were finally pardoned by President Lincoln.

When he was released, and returned to the new reservation upon the Missouri river, he soon became convinced that life on a government reservation meant physical and moral degradation. Therefore he determined, with several others, to try the white man's way of gaining a livelihood. They accordingly left the agency against the persuasions of the agent, renounced all government assistance, and took land under the United States Homestead law, on the Big Sioux river. After he had made his home there, he desired to seek his lost child. It was then a dangerous undertaking to cross the line, but his Christian love prompted him to do it. He secured a good guide, and found his way in time through the vast wilderness.

As for me, I little dreamed of anything unusual to happen on my return. As I approached our camp with my game on my shoulder, I had not the slightest premonition that I was suddenly to be hurled from my savage life into a life unknown to me hitherto.

When I appeared in sight my father, who had patiently listened to my uncle's long account of my early life and training, became very much excited. He was eager to embrace the child who, as he had just been informed, made it already the object of his life to avenge his father's blood. The loving father could not remain in the teepee and watch the boy coming, so he started to meet him. My uncle arose to go with his brother to insure his safety.

My face burned with the unusual excitement caused by the sight of a man wearing the Big Knives' clothing and coming toward me with my uncle.

"What does this mean, uncle?"

"My boy, this is your father, my brother, whom we mourned as dead. He has come for you."

My father added: "I am glad that my son is strong and brave. Your brothers have adopted the white man's way; I came for you to learn this new way, too; and I want you to grow up a good man."

He had brought me some civilized clothing, At first, I disliked very much to wear garments made by the people I had hated so bitterly. But the thought that, after all, they had not killed my father and brothers, reconciled me, and I put on the clothes.

In a few days we started for the States. I felt as if I were dead and traveling to the Spirit Land; for now all my old ideas were to give place to new ones, and my life was to be entirely different from that of the past.

Still, I was eager to see some of the wonderful inventions of the white people. When we reached Fort Totten, I gazed about me with lively interest and a quick imagination.

My father had forgotten to tell me that the fire-boat-walks-on-mountains had its track at Jamestown, and might appear at any moment. As I was watering the ponies, a peculiar shrilling noise pealed forth from just beyond the hills. The ponies threw back their heads and listened; then they ran snorting over the prairie. Meanwhile, I too had taken alarm. I leaped on the back of one of the ponies, and dashed off at full speed. It was a clear day; I could not imagine what had caused such an unearthly noise. It seemed as if the world were about to burst in two!

I got upon a hill as the train appeared. "O!" I said to myself, "that is the fire-boat-walkson-mountains that I have heard about!" Then I drove back the ponies.

My father was accustomed every morning to read from his Bible, and sing a stanza of a hymn. I was about very early with my gun for several mornings; but at last he stopped me as I was preparing to go out, and bade me wait.

I listened with much astonishment. The hymn contained the word Jesus. I did not comprehend what this meant; and my father then told me that Jesus was the Son of God who came on earth to save sinners, and that it was because of him that he had sought me. This conversation made a deep impression upon my mind.

Late in the fall we reached the citizen settlement at Flandreau, South Dakota, where my father and some others dwelt among the whites. Here my wild life came to an end, and my school days began.

A Note About the Author

Charles A. Eastman (1858–1939) was a Santee Dakota physician, lecturer, activist, and writer. Born Hakadah in Minnesota, he was the last of five children of Mary Nancy Eastman, a woman of mixed racial heritage who died shortly after giving birth. Separated from his father and siblings during the Dakota War of 1862, Eastman—who later earned the name Ohíye S'a—was raised by his maternal grandmother in North Dakota and Manitoba. Fifteen years later, he was reunited with his father and oldest brother—who were presumed dead—in South Dakota. At his father's encouragement, Ohíye S'a converted to Christianity and took the name Charles Alexander Eastman, which he would use for the rest of his life. Educated at Dartmouth College, Eastman enrolled in Boston University's medical program after graduating in 1897. He completed his medical degree in 1890, making him one of the first Native Americans to do so. Eastman then moved back to South Dakota, where he worked as a physician for the Bureau of Indian Affairs at the Pine Ridge and Crow Creek Reservations. During a period of economic hardship, he used his wife Elaine Goodale's encouragement to write stories about his childhood, a few of which found publication in *St. Nicholas Magazine*. In 1902, he published *Memories of an Indian Boyhood*, a memoir about his life among the Dakota Sioux. In addition to his writing, Eastman maintained a private medical practice, helped establish the Boy Scouts of America, worked as a spokesman for the YMCA and Carlisle Indian Industrial School, and acted as an advisor to several Presidential administrations.

A Note from the Publisher

Spanning many genres, from non-fiction essays to literature classics to children's books and lyric poetry, Mint Edition books showcase the master works of our time in a modern new package. The text is freshly typeset, is clean and easy to read, and features a new note about the author in each volume. Many books also include exclusive new introductory material. Every book boasts a striking new cover, which makes it as appropriate for collecting as it is for gift giving. Mint Edition books are only printed when a reader orders them, so natural resources are not wasted. We're proud that our books are never manufactured in excess and exist only in the exact quantity they need to be read and enjoyed.